PRAISE FOR
Hitman-Baker-Casketmaker:
Aftermath of an American's Clash with ICE

Winner of the 2020 Midwest Book Award for General Poetry
2019 Shelf Unbound Best Indie Book Competition: Notable 100

"Klecko's affection and respect for his crew spill out onto the pages."
—Lee Svitak Dean, *Star Tribune*

"Klecko cuts a memorable figure. He's tall, and has been known to train in a boxing gym. An impressive array of tattoos covers his arms and legs. Klecko says he doesn't have the answers but people need to talk about who is providing their daily bread."
—Euan Kerr, Minnesota Public Radio

"This is a memorable collection. These are Henry Miller poems in a rough language that makes even Frank O'Hara seem delicate and lyrical."
—Joel Van Valin, editor of *Whistling Shade*

"Illegal immigrants can't bother with renown. At least, not the kind that a Paris-destined baker, or a poet, or a novelist might chase. And yet, in *Hitman*, Klecko finds it most fitting to immortalize the moments and people who typically go unsung."
—Erik Tormoen, *Minnesota Monthly*

"Klecko probably doesn't look like the first guy you'd expect to write a book of verse probing our national immigration question from a first-hand perspective."   —Drew Wood, *Mpls. St. Paul Magazine*

"Klecko—a baker who writes poems. A friend with integr⋯ ⋯ ⋯ human being. An award-winning author. This is so fuckin⋮
—David Fhima, world-ren⋯

"People in the industry know that bakers tend to be a spiritu⋯ of our most philosophical has to be the St. Paul baker that g⋯ name: Klecko. He's written for years about the industry a⋯ life for different publications, but his new work is very per⋯ important."   —Stephanie March, *Mpls. St. Pau⋯*

LINCOLNLAND

Other books by Klecko

Hitman-Baker-Casketmaker:
Aftermath of an American's Clash with ICE
Out for a Lark
The Bluebeard of Happiness
A Pox Upon Your Blessings
Houdini in St. Paul
My British Hindu Bible
Robert Bly and the Monk in His Cell
Mayor 4 Life
Brando Land

LINCOLNLAND

Danny Klecko's Pandemic Diary

By Klecko

PARIS MORNING
PUBLICATIONS

Published in 2021 by Paris Morning Publications
www.parismorningpublications.com

Copyright © Paris Morning Publications

Published and printed in the United States of America
ISBN: 978-0-578-84475-6

Cover design by Audrey Campbell
www.ataudrey.com

"Klecko accomplished more in a pandemic year than most people do in a lifetime."

—Julie Pfitzinger,

TO THE WRITERS OF THE APOCALYPSE

George Saunders
Leif Enger
Jonathan Franzen
Sjón

As you can imagine
I'm in your debt
This book is dedicated to you
In friendship

—Klecko

TO THE WRITERS WHO KNEW ME NOT

Karl Ove Knausgård
James McBride
Rumaan Alam
Gloria Steinem

Since you chose
Not to participate
In my pandemic
I only thought it fair
To inform my Tribe
This book is not
Dedicated to you

No hard feelings

—Klecko

LINCOLNLAND

JEREMIAH 29:13

KJV

"And ye shall seek me
And find me
When ye shall search for me
With all your heart"

DEAR DIARY

After losing my clash with ICE
After losing the bakery
After losing the Super Bowl bread contracts
After losing my . . .
Purpose, reputation and crew
I wasn't sure what to do
So I wrote a little book of poems
Called . . .
HITMAN-BAKER-CASKETMAKER
I wanted to fight back
But, I was alone
Absent from the Tribe
I didn't know how to proceed
Until . . .
I had the dream

LINCOLN DREAM

High noon, the prairie was deserted
Sitting alone at the Park & Ride
Tick–Tock, the sun was blaring
Tick–Tock, I was sad
Zoom, a pickup pulled in and circled twice
It was Abraham Lincoln
Wearing jeans and an Izod polo
Containing the new logo, without the crocodile
That disappointed him by his own admission
Without ceremony, he hopped in my car
Without hesitation, he reminded me
How familiar he was with tabloids and slander
How painful it was watching loved ones suffer
We sat in silence, for a long time
Until Lincoln said . . .
I followed your story
Your crew got fucked, hard
So, where's your focus, healing or vindication
I answered . . . vodka, he smiled and reminded me
As long as your body has breath, it has hope
Let's shoot for vindication
You're going to need a big platform
Come out to DC, I'm easy to find

SQUIRREL & CROW

Whatever action proceeds pandemonium
Is exactly what occurred
Outside, by the donut dumpster
In front of me, a German and an African
Stood despondent, staring at the squirrel
Who died, clinging to the dumpster
Trying to pull itself out
It should have escaped easily
I've never seen anything dead, look so alive
Above, perched a crow, big as a terrier
Cawing with unprecedented volume
The German wondered, would the crow swoop down
And vulture the rodent corpse
None of us liked that idea much
And considered placing the squirrel
Inside the dumpster and closing the lid
Until the African mused thoughtfully
Perhaps it would be best, to let it be
Its brothers and sisters are probably looking for him
They deserve to know
We returned to the bakery
Finishing our shift with heavy hearts

OZ—1

It never occurred to me, shutting down a business
Could be harder than launching one
Unloading equipment, pennies on the dollar
Affection disconnected, purpose dismantled
The younger employees would be ok
Time was on their side
But for those of us, the older bakers
Starting tomorrow, we would join the ranks
Of former All Stars, clinging to dignity during
     our descent
Like Michael Jordon with the Washington Wizards
Maybe it would be better to fade away, go out on top
The only thing that kept me afloat was the flavor of vodka
As I rolled over, the Russian Supermodel was smiling
Russian Supermodels seldom smile while dreaming
Unless the dreams reveal Nazis losing, orphans reunited
Or ice cream
I took this to be a positive omen and drifted off to sleep
Knowing in five hours, I would experience . . .
My first, first day on the job
In over 3o years

On the second day of my new job
I was called out of production
Into the human resource office
Where a woman with a man's name
Stared at me, then the floor
Announcing, E-Verify wouldn't clear me
They claimed I wasn't in legal standing
As I plead my innocence, humiliation joined me
As the woman with the man's name
Said she hoped it was a misunderstanding
While briefly casting a glance, which led me to believe
She wouldn't be surprised
If I was involved in something notorious
Immediately an appeal was filed
For several days, I remained red flagged
For several days, I received inquisitive looks
Eventually, when I was cleared
I asked E-Verify what evidence they had against me
The representative laughed
Told me it wasn't my concern, and hung up
Even though my name was cleared
I still couldn't help feeling
I had ended up . . .
On the wrong side of the rainbow

OZ—3

(A Smithsonian Postmortem)
They weren't actually red
But more of a burgundy
Otherwise Technicolor
Would have made them fluorescent orange
They weren't actually ruby
Sequins were glued in place
This made the footwear lighter
Not to mention cost effective
A sign behind velvet ropes explained
Three other pairs existed
Each set of slippers
Created for specific duties
She stared into the case
Remained silent
I wondered if such functionality
Crippled a lifetime of fantasy
Not a word was spoken
As we exited the exhibit
Until we stepped outside
And she announced . . .
That was spectacular

What you learn working a trade show booth next to
    Mickey Carroll
At 18 he appeared in shows with Mae West
While under contract with MGM
He went to school with Judy Garland and Mickey Rooney
It was Garland who invited him onto the Oz set
He marched as a Munchkin soldier
And was the candy-striped fiddler
Who escorted Dorothy down the yellow brick road
After retiring, he worked charities
To raise money for the St. Louis Police Department
This is where he met Cardinals slugger, Mark McGwire
The two men became friends
When asked . . .
If calling him a Munchkin was politically incorrect
He responded . . .
You are what you are
And I am a Munchkin

Grand Rapids, Minnesota
The All-American Girl invited me onto her radio show
After I told her things she liked
She invited me to host a festival
At a place past nowhere
At a place on the edge of the map
At a place you'd assume
Might be the muse for every Norman Rockwell painting
In the town square, everyone ate ice cream
In the town square, folks held organized tadpole races
Off the highway, at the motel
Plastic swipe keys hadn't been discovered
Guests received big keys
Like the ones marshals use to lock jail cells
Off the highway, on a house
A sign announced Judy Garland Museum
If that didn't pique tourists' curiosity
Underneath that was a banner asking
Who stole the ruby slippers

If we were a Norman Rockwell painting
I imagine our likeness would be captured
Outside an ice cream shop
In ideal weather
Where I would find comfort
In the predictability
Of ordering a vanilla cone
You on the other hand
Would place your faith
In flavors never sampled
Knowing that after one lick
If your eyes announced disappointment
I would swap you my vanilla
For the thousandth time

OZ—7

Inside the Judy Garland Museum
My companion was captivated
Stopping to read every placard
The information underwhelmed me
I was hoping to see artifacts pertaining to flying monkeys
Not dresses, socks and the bed Frances Gumm slept in
My companion was in heaven
She waited a lifetime for this
I on the other hand . . .
My companion became bothered by my boredom
Therefore advising me, to go back to the gift shop
Where she would join me later
And possibly buy me a refrigerator magnet
If I could simply manage
Not to ruin this perfect moment

According to the Toto poster . . .

- She was a she, a Cairn Terrier named Terry, born in Chicago
- Before Oz, Toto starred in "Bright Eyes" with Shirley Temple
- Toto was paid more than the Munchkins
- A Winkie guardsman stepped on Toto's foot . . . X-rays revealed a break, a stunt double was needed . . . Garland became her personal attendant
- After the film, Garland tried to adopt Toto, she failed
- Toto appeared in more scenes than Dorothy
- After the Wizard of Oz, Terry's name was changed to Toto
- In 1945, Toto died at the age of 13 She was buried at the home of her trainer
- In 1958, the Ventura Freeway was developed And runs over Toto's grave to this day

Inside the Judy Garland gift shop
At a speed set to hypnotize
A carriage was displayed
The carriage that ferried Dorothy
And her entourage into the Emerald City
Drawn by the horse of a different color
A placard explained . . .
It was used in 199 Hollywood films
Including John Wayne's last picture
My mind processed, my sightline focused
On a cardboard cutout of Abraham Lincoln
A placard explained . . .
The carriage was made for him
To be used during the Civil War

Heading back to the Sawmill Inn
Topics important to no one but us were discussed
Such as refrigerator magnets
She chose Glinda the good witch
I chose flying monkeys
After encouraging each other's selections
The carriage was discussed
I pointed out, the plaque on the chassis said
A. Lincoln June 8th 1863
I was born July 8th 1963
I announced, separated by a century and a month
Exactly . . .
Then I asked if that meant anything
It seemed like it should
Without hesitation, she replied . . . no
Then she smiled and wondered
If it was important for me
To find a way to connect to Lincoln
Then I smiled and wondered
Before answering . . . maybe

SODAK—1

There I stood
My lens pointed in the face of George Washington
The red light blinked, my camera battery was dead
I needed a replacement
At the foot of Mount Rushmore
Rests a small cluster of buildings
Consisting of restaurants and an ice cream stand
And . . . a souvenir store
I entered, only to become overwhelmed
By countless trinkets and souvenirs
Velvet pillows, key chains
Snow globes and shot glasses
It was simultaneously tacky
And somewhat impressive
I walked through every aisle
Like I was circling the drain
But when I arrived at the center
Everything changed

SODAK—2

Resting against a foldout table
Sat Dan "Nick" Clifford
Placed in front of him was a pile
Of his recent book about working
On the Mount Rushmore monument
Between 1938 and 1940
To his left stood his wife
Waving people over
Like a carnival barker, barking . . .
Come on over, meet the last living sculptor
That carved the face of Abraham Lincoln
A small group of young boys approached
As the wife continued a step-by-step
Account of her husband's legend
Nick showed the kid
With a Baltimore Orioles T-shirt
How to grip the laces
When throwing a curveball

As the child attempted to mimic this
Nick reminisced out loud . . .
Mr. Borglum gave me this job
He started this project
He was a big fan of baseball
He saw me pitching
When my squad made it to the state finals
When he learned I lived in Keystone
He was kind enough to offer me a job
What most people don't know is
Our Rushmore workers had a baseball team
And I became their pitcher

SODAK—4

Shoving the kids aside, I addressed the man . . .
C'mon Nick, do you expect me to believe
You slipped into a harness
And dangled off the side of a mountain
Just so you could play ball
The old man smiled at my ignorance
Before explaining . . .
Prior to that, I worked in the mines
The mines are worse than the mountain
Far worse
Back then a guy felt fortunate
To have a job
Any job

SODAK—5

When the kid in the Orioles shirt
Finally got the proper grip on the baseball
He released it and asked
How old are you, Nick
91 years old, son
For a split second, I noticed
How the old man and the boy
Looked at each other
As if wishing
They could change places
A woman in white sunglasses interrupted . . .
Nick, did you or the other workers
Feel like you were creating art

SODAK—6

No ma'am, none of us did
This was just considered a job
But then, years back
Back when the monument
Celebrated its 5oth anniversary
President Bush came out here
To give a presentation
That was a big deal
Many workers flew cross country
To unite for this moment

SODAK—7

I think maybe it was then
We all understood the magnitude
Or importance
Of what Mr. Borglum had accomplished
Every 4th of July after that
We held a reunion
Everyone felt very fortunate
To take part in something
People care about, the world over
It amazes me
Every day, if you come here
You have the opportunity
To meet some of the nicest people
From across the planet

SODAK—8

Finally
The woman in white sunglasses
Asked Nick's wife
If Nick felt a responsibility
To be present, since . . .
He was the only person left
Who could give a firsthand account
Of how Mount Rushmore came to be
Nick's wife nodded slowly
Sharing that he plans to stay
On the mountain
For the rest of his life
So he can share the experiences
And stories
Of the many colleagues
He was fortunate to work with

SODAK—9

Just as he said this . . .
I saw another small boy approach the table
To learn how to grip the curveball
And that's when it occurred to me
That maybe . . .
My country's most amazing
Surviving mountain carver
Just liked chatting up baseball

MINNESOTA'S BEST BOOK CRITIC—1

Meet Mary Ann Grossmann
At 81, she's just begun to hit her stride
Reviewing books at the Pioneer Press
For what . . . half a century, plus or minus
Once I asked . . .
Do you read the classics
You're expected to review what's new
She answered . . .
I never read the classics
But, sometimes I treat myself
To James Herriot
This makes sense
Knowing she lives in a cottage
With more strays than Dr. Dolittle
Once I asked . . .
Would you like to read
At the Turf Club
At the Bukowski Tribute
She paused before asking . . .
Can I read a cat poem

At the Turf Club, in the basement, the Clown Lounge
I thanked everyone for coming
To the Bukowski Tribute
But, before releasing the audience
I introduced the evening's final guest
Mary Ann Grossmann
Who inched toward the microphone
Where she smiled and announced . . .
It's good to end with a cat poem
Especially when it's titled
ONE TOUGH MOTHERFUCKER
During the last stanza
When the press ask Bukowski
If he was inspired by French poets
He picked up his cat and said . . .
I'm inspired by this, by this . . .
My cross-eyed, toothless
Shot, run over, no tailed friend
Grossmann couldn't contain her joy
So, she said goodnight
The crowd exploded
And St. Paul was merry once more

Although unethical
Hunting leprechauns still exists in St. Paul
A city filled with Irish
A city where honest people
Feel entitled to their pot of gold
I set my stakeout in the Kwik Trip parking lot
If tradition held true, I still had 3o minutes
Before mayhem ensued
Inside Kwik Trip, I bought Red Bull and a Pioneer Press
Inside my car, I toasted St. Patrick's Day
By drinking instant energy and opening the newspaper
There it was, there I was, staring back at me
Pixelated, eight inches square
God Bless Mary Ann Grossmann
Reviewing my book, promoting my launch
I remembered our phone conversation
And how she predicted, my little book of poems
Was certain to cause big problems for ICE
This was enough to help me realize
The leprechauns could keep their treasure
I already had mine
And thus began the . . .
HITMAN-BAKER-CASKETMAKER
Tour

If my publisher hadn't twisted my arm
I wouldn't have attended
The only thing more disheartening
Than standing amidst 1000 writers
Is standing amidst 1000 writers with MFAs
They smell desperate, look uncertain
Wearing masks that announce
They wish they were somebody other than themselves
God Bless Mary Ann Grossmann
She found out the event's main speaker
Was Linda Boström Knausgård
She reminded me that she remembered
How much I loved Nordic authors
Then asked if I wanted to review her newest book
For the Pioneer Press
At the event, Boström sought me out
Thanked me for my praise
Then we stood awkwardly in silence
She mentioned, she heard I was a writer
I responded . . . no, I'm a baker
She inched closer
To discuss topics you don't need to consider

DRY TORTUGA—1

Splish–Splash, waves crash
Starboard side of our oceanic shuttle
Park Ranger sits across from us
But talks to her, about all things
Pertaining to Dr. Samuel Mudd
He mentions . . . we'll see the doctor's cell
He mentions . . . prison epidemic and heroic deeds
Deeds brave enough to issue pardon
To a man implicated
In conspiring to kill President Lincoln
A shuttle steward interrupts
Offering a roast beef, turkey or veggie option
Park Ranger waves him past
And talks to us, talks to her, and lets her know
Half his peeps think Mudd was innocent
The other half, disagree
Splish–Splash, she calls the steward back
And orders the turkey before asking . . .
What do you think, innocent or guilty
The Park Ranger stalls, then answers with fact
Were you aware, a crocodile swims around the island
He's the only croc to inhabit these waters
In over a century

DRY TORTUGA—2

In silence exists a brick prison
On an island
Closer to Cuba than Florida
In silence, it's encircled by a walkway
Which also serves as a moat enclosure
Our shuttle docks, tourists disembark
Bringing noise to a place
That may have been paradise moments prior
Tourists rush, tourists pass
She sits, squints and dangles her legs over the moat
We are alone, waves crush in rhythm
I may have been in a trance
When I asked . . .
Should we go on to Havana
In a neutral tone, she reminded me
Why consider options
When you're in the midst of beauty
The moment the rebuke passed her lips
The croc surfaced
And stared at her
Until they addressed each other
With smiles that were nearly identical

ON THE MORNING OF MY 56TH BIRTHDAY

Mother and I sat in the café
She asked about book sales
How things were going in general
I confessed, it occurred to me recently
I wasn't ashamed that ICE broke me
Odds are long when you wrestle Nazis
But the local municipalities
We served them for decades
Now when they pass by
I go unnoticed, as if I were Ebenezer Scrooge
Trapped in a Christmas dream
Mother smiled and explained
Cheer up kiddo, you won't need to worry
Things will get sorted out, eventually
In the 6os, everybody talked about the future
How the world would go global
Everybody seemed to think global was the key
But, they didn't explain why
And now that it's finally happened
Nobody knows what to do
But I have every confidence
You will find your solution

ST. AGNES IN THE BARDO

Never in my life
Have I visited a gravesite
Spoke more than briefly to a ghost
Or found myself attached to sentiment
Yet . . . more days than not
I leave my natural course
And find myself parked
In front of what once was
St. Agnes Baking Company
Only for a minute
Staring into darkness has become routine
Staring at the vacant space seems necessary
On paper, this may seem disturbing
But, the action is the result of loss
When a wife leaves you, or a dog dies
You disconnect from the heart
But when you lose your crew
You become disconnected . . .
From your art and purpose

GEORGE SAUNDERS—1

Klecko—Your Wikipedia page said you subscribe
   to brevity
You prefer Hemingway and Raymond Carver
However . . . I found BARDO fast and overlapping
I was off-balance in the best way
The characters had eastern sensibilities
I would have never guessed
This was written by a Texan

George—I was born in Texas, Amarillo
We only stayed a year
Before moving to the south side of Chicago
To answer your question
Yeah, the book was weird for me
I've been a Buddhist for 30 years
That got mixed in with the historic text
There's a lot of characters
So, I developed a compressed style
And did my best
To make sure "my" writing didn't stick out
It came together, when I relaxed

Klecko—Other than Christ, more books have
   been written
About Lincoln than anyone else
Last year I was at Subtext Books
Talking to some Lincoln nerds, our consensus was . . .
Lincoln likes your book the most
*Unique format
*The tribute goes to Willie
Lincoln loved him most
You know he loved this gesture
*When Bardo residents hopped into Lincoln
He unified more than flesh
He unified their souls
In my opinion
That passage was the crowning moment
Not only of your career
But of all literature
Ever . . .
It's beautiful
Nobody will ever top that

George—The people who entered Lincoln
Was a response to an accident
In the first crypt scene
When Willie leans on Lincoln
I had to look past metaphysical
And determine, what actually happens
When spirit and flesh collide
I became delighted considering the option
It was a long messy process
Lots of rewriting
But that gave me opportunities
One thing for sure, concerning Lincoln
I didn't need a person
I wanted a dynamic
Abe only came in when necessary
Equally important . . .
I knew I had to get him out
Quick as possible

Klecko—Lincoln was influenced by dreams
Are you, was BARDO

George—No, it's a ghost story, ghost lore
Actually, the book doesn't have
A lot of Bardo scenes
But there is some . . .
"Beetlejuice"
Dante's Inferno
I enjoyed using Autumn
Autumn is spooky
The form unlocked

Klecko—Let's go back to crescendo
When the Bardo residents enter Lincoln's body
Spirits are unified, understanding was magnified
It's a powerful passage
Was this the original idea that launched the concept

George—No, I've lived in Illinois, everything is Lincoln
    there
I've been to the tomb, I saw where Willie was buried
I used to be an engineer
Often times I think of different ways
To get to the same place
The question was, how many times would Lincoln
    appear
And where would I place the crypt scenes
The first time, he left at the worst time
Nothing was resolved
I needed one more scene
I had to slow things down
Truth is . . . I didn't want to do Oliver Stone
I didn't want theories
I didn't want debate

GEORGE SAUNDERS—6

George—When the souls jumped in Lincoln
They started off sad
The Bardo is a sad place
Kind of like a nursing home
Where old people repeat the same stories
In an attempt to remain relevant
Think about it, they have to be narcissistic
If their purpose is going to maintain value
When the souls hopped in
They helped Willie
They helped someone other than themselves
That to me . . . was the human act
An act that would return them
To their former glory

Klecko—Did any part of you
Write this book for Lincoln

George—No, not really
I felt he would love it
A crazy preacher sent me an e-mail
Chastising me for making money
By exploiting Abe and Willie
But, you know . . .
Throughout Bardo, I kept pictures
Of Lincoln and Willie
In my writing area, to remind me
They're not literary play things
I'm a dad
I know what love feels like
In that way, I honored him
That's a form of love

GEORGE SAUNDERS—8

Klecko—Many people connected to Lincoln's purpose
Have seen his ghost
Or felt his presence, have you

George—No, no, no . . .
I've been in his graveyard
In a way, I was struck by his presence
It made me think
Of what he did, right and wrong
Life can go from neurotic to smooth
In seconds
If you snap, do something stupid
Say something you shouldn't
It's important to remember
These things aren't carved in stone
Every moment is a restart
That's what I thought about
In the graveyard

Klecko—I have already established
I believe . . .
LINCOLN IN THE BARDO
Is the smartest novel ever written
And I told you . . .
My friends, the Lincoln nerds
We all agree
Lincoln likes your depiction the best . . .
I'm not one who asks often, George
But . . .
I'd be crazy not to
In this instance
How can I make my Lincoln book
Better than yours

GEORGE SAUNDERS—10

George—(Laughing) (pausing)
(More pausing)
For me, I'm a big rewriter
It's my golden ticket
In this process, you become aware
Of your micro preferences
While micro preferencing, the revision sits up
And your lame ass ideas
Get pushed aside
The best book about Lincoln
Will never be about Lincoln
It has to be about you
To get there, you'll need intuition
And the wisdom of a rock climber
Or somebody who knows
How to hit the curveball

RASPBERRY ISLAND—1

When the wind exceeds 20 mph
When your kite hits 300 feet
When your line surpasses taut
Making a noise, between hum and scream
At this point . . . the flight is secondary
At this point . . . it's all about the tug
When I feel this
One of two things occur
Either I go into a trance
Or find myself remembering moments
Likely to remain forgotten

RASPBERRY ISLAND—2

Above the island, kite extended
I thought of New York
How we arrived early
The hotel wouldn't let us check in
You took me uptown
To a Madison Avenue art gallery
Displaying Diane Arbus photographs
Gallery attendants appeared to be in a lather
With their mouths closed
In positions suggesting rebuke
My phone rang
A short attendant with long dreadlocks
Gave me the look
You know the look . . .
He rolled his eyes . . .
Hissed and sighed
I inched in, placing him in shadow
Before explaining . . .
If Arbus was here
She'd love me, and we would hate you
Dreadlocks looked frightened, then sad
Then I felt sad, and became frightened

Accusing Diane Arbus . . .
Because it's in your nature
To point cameras at lost souls
Click—little boy and hand grenade
Click—dwarf without a tribe
Click—man applying makeup in secret
Individually, these photographs intrigue me
But viewed in succession
I become overwhelmed and uncomfortable
By, beautiful people, isolated
By, beautiful people, disconnected
Each time I close your book
I wonder, would things have been different
If I had been your boyfriend
That's why, if I ever stumble upon Aladdin's lamp
You have my full assurance
That I will use one of my wishes
To unite us in a church-basement kitchen
Where we will make fruit salad
With Nuns and optimistic Lutherans
And at the end of the night, if you still want to die
We'll stay with you
So you won't have to cross alone

RASPBERRY ISLAND—4

Alone on the island, kite extended
I found comfort in isolation
Until, I saw . . . it
A speck on the horizon
I paid no attention, until I did
The speck turned into a man
A man larger than me, dragging a duffel
He didn't veer, left or right
He walked directly toward me
I prepared for battle, but . . .
He stopped, waved, and produced a kite
For a million years, we stood together silent
Until my new friend asked . . .
Is there anything better
I shook my head no
Then he asked . . .
Is there a way to let the world
Know what they're missing
To which I answered . . .
How about a poem or short story
Duffel guy responded without flinching
Nah, that would be stupid

Alone on an island, kite extended
I remembered the Bicentennial
How fantastic it was, even though . . .
I was determined to ruin it for everyone
On July 4th, I wanted to stay home
Sneak whiskey, smoke cigs and talk to girls
I was 13, double-dosed on testosterone
Instead, I ended up at Jellystone Park
With pow-wows, aqua ducks
And a 30-foot statue of Yogi Bear
In our tent, mother sought refuge
In her television and makeup mirror
I was ashamed and became a campground orphan
I met Mindy, or Molly, she was 15
And wanted to show me her boobs
Explaining they were identical
To the boobs on the Farrah Fawcett poster
I became nervous and offered, blondes were passé
On my closet, I had a poster of Patty Hearst

RASPBERRY ISLAND—6

I like you Patty Hearst . . .
If time allowed an edit
I would join you in the closet
To marvel at your features
In less than perfect darkness
But maybe we should whisper
As they fumble through the ransom
Which they can keep for all I care
While we share the closet
Where you will tell me stories
Of conversations long forgotten
Just as long as I promise
Not to follow when you leave
And you won't have to worry
Because I don't want a lifetime
I only want a moment
To have you in the closet

RASPBERRY ISLAND—7

We stood isolated, prepared
Sloggers, slickers, hoodies and hats
She the pilot, me the technician
Mentioning, when we're here
We are at our best
She told me a secret
Days are too long
Nothing changes
But, when you have reason to look up
Things make sense
Our definition of us, of who we are
Can't be completed with union
It's not enough
We require wind

DEAR DIARY—1

When your book is announced
The flavor of the moment
The unthinkable happens
People buy it, read it
Sometimes, they come out in droves
To see why you are, who you are
That way . . . they can define it
Own it, own you, I don't mind . . .
Until I do
Book stores, book clubs
Turn the page . . .
Beer halls and cocktail lounges
Turn the page . . .
I read to a baker's dozen
At the East Side Freedom Library
I read to 1014 foodservice workers
At the Pantages Theatre
Book sales were up
But, my spirit was down
Where was Lincoln
Vindication had eluded me
Where was Lincoln

DEAR DIARY—2

The last leg, of the first half of the tour
Finished at Moon Palace Books
The show ended, chit-chat, gab & gush
The crowd rose and tangled
While the baker slipped out
To examine books in the storefront
I was looking for . . .
MONTANA 1948 by Larry Watson
But, my pursuit was curtailed
By my publisher who pursued me
I knew what she wanted
I gulped
She said . . . you've been ditching me
Enough, we need to tack down
Venues and dates to finish the tour
I explained I was looking for MONTANA 1948
She rolled her eyes
And brought me to the counter
Where she bought me a copy of EVENTIDE
A novel by Kent Haruf
Insisting it was a better book
Insisting I better call the following day

DEAR DIARY—3

Ring–Ring, the publisher answered
I don't know how to say this . . . said Klecko
So, I'll just tell you the truth
Awhile back, I had a dream
Abraham Lincoln promised he would help me
To be more specific, he didn't promise
His ghost did
But he said I had to go to DC
And once I get there, he'll make himself known
I'm done reading in Minnesota
I'm taking my message to the nation's capital
If you can help me . . . great
But either way . . .
I have to find Lincoln's ghost
Tap–Tap–Tap drummed the publisher's pen
Creating a nervous rhythm
Then . . . silence
Then . . . let's talk tomorrow
Then . . . good night

DEAR DIARY—4

Several days passed, the publisher didn't call
She usually calls, but on this day
She sent an e-mail

Dear Klecko,
I got you a reading engagement at the Potter's House
It's in a tougher part of DC
The venue is historic, steeped in social justice
I believe they've been around close to 50 years
They are nice people, smart people
Attached is flight information
And lodging particulars
I booked you three nights at the Architect Hotel
Meaning . . .
Push books for me one day
And that will give you two more
To track down Lincoln's ghost
Best of luck . . .
Julie

SEATTLE—1

After mentioning I would be heading to DC in six weeks
After mentioning I needed to go alone
I issued an invitation to the Russian Super Model . . .
Do the math, subtract my earning power from my age
Even though I lost the bakery and hit a financial pothole
I still have enough money . . .
To take you any place on the planet
London, Paris, Reykjavik or Rome
Gosh . . .
We could even head back to Maui
Where do you want to go . . .
She thought about it
Every bit of 3o seconds
Before responding . . .
Seattle

SEATTLE—2

Dateline—Pier 57
She's never liked Ferris wheels
This one was 175 feet tall
She said . . . never in a million years
Unless, I bought ice cream
Across from us, in our gondola
Sat a family from Dubai
A father, his daughter, and her new husband
The first time up, at the top
The young man began to cower
The second time, the father shook his head
Teasing the daughter, her husband was afraid
The final time we reached the top
The father looked at me and shrugged
I explained . . . I too have a son-in-law
And his favorite food is peach crepes
We didn't laugh
Instead . . .
We shared a glance of understanding

SEATTLE—3

Across the intersection, a girl and her bike
Leaning in such a way, it was hard to tell
Which one propped the other
The light turned green, everyone advanced
Except her . . .
As I drew closer, she hung her head
But her eyes remained looking upward
Presenting a sadness tears couldn't help
As I passed . . .
She spoke softly into the phone . . .
Are you mad at me
The tone she used was hollow
Hollow enough that I determined
The person on the other line couldn't be mad
They were disappointed
That's when it occurred to me
This wasn't a lovers' spat
The pain seemed deeper
She had to have been talking to her mother

SEATTLE—4

Project—Bird & French Fry
He introduced himself as Calvin
From Boston
Enthused to offer me dominion over the world
For only three dollars
I usually don't bite, but this time I did
Certain he would vanish with the money
Instead, he returned with French fries
And scattered them across the pavement
Before telling me to wait
So we waited, awhile, or just a bit longer
Until a small bird landed
Dancing over French fries
Burying its beak into potato greatness
Delighted, I snapped photos
Until Calvin reminded me . . .
A guy can spread a lot of joy
When he's in control of resources
And does the right thing

SEATTLE—5

Project—Bird & French Fries
Captain America bounced, peddling his rickshaw
Additional birds gathered
Finishing off French fry remnants
Calvin stood silent
Until pointing to the Great Wheel, announcing . . .
It's 175 feet high, tallest on the coast
I mentioned I rode it
With a family from Dubai
Calvin looked up, then down
Confessing he never had the pleasure
I usually don't bite, but this time I did
Offering to pay our admissions
Calvin reminded me, for the same price
We could get four beers . . . each
Point taken . . . I responded
I have more money than time
Somewhere there's a Russian Super Model
Waking from a nap
Calvin told me not to keep her waiting
Before shaking my hand
And telling me to hustle back
The very moment, we finished our first round

SEATTLE—6

Dateline—Puget Sound
With time enough
To create a final memory
We stared toward the water
Leaned against chain link
She, had the posture of a person
Who seldom made gestures
We stood silent, and silent
And silent, until . . .
A blue balloon passed overhead
I looked at her, the balloon
And back at her
She offered me her hand and asked
If I was nervous about DC
I nodded yes
There was a pause, until she released my hand
And pointed to the balloon, asking . . .
You know what that means, right . . .
I nodded no, so she explained . . .
Starting tomorrow
The world is going to turn over
A new leaf

DC—1

Lee Svitak Dean is . . .
The most powerful person in Minnesota
Our state's gatekeeper
Of all things culinary
How many decades has she . . .
Edited the Strib's TASTE section
During our phone conversation
We discussed restaurant closings
Her event at the American Swedish Institute
And her opportunity to throw out the opening pitch
At a Minnesota Twins game
Before hanging up
She asked about my book tour
I mentioned I was taking it to DC
She mentioned she could get me publicity
If I wanted . . . I wanted
Said yes, then little else
It can be hard, for me at least
To express love, and gratitude
To the most powerful person in Minnesota

NOTE TO SELF . . .
When you get featured in the Washington Post
When their top food critic
Gives your book a big thumb's up
Buckle up buttercup, life will never be the same
People will love you
People will hate you
But, after the Chicago Tribune
And dozens of newspapers
From cities you've never heard of
Pick the story up off the AP wire
Nothing matters, nothing matters
Nothing matters, except . . .
People buy the book
People read the book
Because, if they do . . .
They will know how much I loved my crew
They will know how wonderful life can be
When you stand with Mexicans

DC—3

When I arrived at the Architect Hotel
It was too early to check in
So I went to the National Art Gallery
4000 paintings spread across six acres
I wanted to see them all, but only had 90 minutes
Instead, I picked one
Dora Maar, by Pablo Picasso
Not green fingernails Dora Maar
Not African Mask Dora Maar
But the early one, where she stood naked
Staring away with indifference
To have ample time with her
I had to bypass Matisse and Miro
I even trotted past Jackson Pollock's #1
However, I stopped for an Edward Hopper piece*
Which surprised me, because I don't like him
For stealing Norman Rockwell characters
And placing them in vampire settings
When I found Dora, I stood still
I stared, energy surfaced
As if she was trying to voice displeasure
Or simply remind us all . . .
To be kinder to our muse

*Groundswell

DC—4

THE HEART OF DORA MAAR

God's the true artist, not Pablo Picasso
I traveled his sculpture, last November
The ocean was heaven
Mountains a temple
Such a sight to see
Children of mine, let me define
I want to . . .
God's the true artist, not Pablo Picasso
I traveled his sculpture, and try to remember
The smile was heaven
Approval a temple
Such a place to be
Children of mine, let me define
Me
I want to . . .
Children of mine, let me define
And see
I want to be your masterpiece

DC—5

The night I went to the Lincoln Memorial
It was late, I was drunk
I took a cab, I climbed the steps
The monument was lit
Shadows transformed an ugly man statue
Into a creepy, ugly man statue
I felt bad for thinking that
Until I remembered
Mother learned from her Audubon group
That a yellow cardinal was spotted in Florida
Only one in a million people see it
The bird's beauty is created by genetic imperfection
I wasn't sure how this pertained
But it did
Realizing this, I sat quietly
Waiting to receive my message
Where was Lincoln
Where was Lincoln

DC—6

The show at Potter's House was great
DC was great
I was about to return to St. Paul
A conquering hero
To my publisher's credit
She picked me up at the airport
And when I hopped in her car
She didn't say a word about book sales
Instead, she asked . . .
Did you find Lincoln's ghost
I shook my head no
And we rode in silence
Until she said . . .
Book sales are steady
We made money, so . . .
Don't lose hope
I'll get another event
I'll send you back
You will see Lincoln's ghost
I know it

DC—7

Arrangements were made
A week in DC
A gig at Solid State Bookstore
Then an after-party
At the house of John Surratt
And his mother Mary
Both were convicted for conspiring
To assassinate Lincoln
Now their house, that house
Was a sushi–karaoke bar
Called Wok and Roll
Everything was set, paid for
I could feel it in my bones
This was it, this was it
I was going to connect
With Lincoln's ghost
But just as I was about to leave
The world changed

DC—8

Plague and pandemic
What will I do
What can I do
And, if DC is out
The logical question is
What's in . . .

NODAK—1

Choo–Choo, the whistle screams
As the train, in my dreams
Pulls into a depot in
Somewhere North Dakota
Choo–Choo, upon the halt
Figure forward, tall and gaunt
Lincoln, standing joyous
Amongst bunting, red, white and blue
Amongst the people, frightened and blue
Hope fills his eyes
As he projects from the caboose
A speech entitled . . .
WE COULD BE HAPPY
Choo–Choo, in my mind
Waking up
Looking for pencil and paper
Wondering if
What is about to be written down
Should be considered plagiarism

NODAK—2

Even if
Just for a moment
Everyone could be happy
I'd play my part
And construct a belfry
Tall and clean
Unattached to any cathedral
Unoccupied by hunchbacks
So, in our brave new world
If you lose your way
As pioneers do
I will ring the bell
For those led off course
By deception and false accounts
And when the chord's pulled taut
Direction will be restored
Not with promises
But tone and echo

FUNERAL TRAIN—1

After President Lincoln was assassinated
His body was repaired
Placed in a train
Shipped from DC to Springfield, Illinois
Like a rock band . . .
The train stopped at numerous destinations
For thousands and thousands of mourners
Like a rock band . . .
Lincoln's body traveled in style
The train was the equivalent to Air Force 1
A team of 300 people accompanied the body
At all times

FUNERAL TRAIN—2

When the tour ended
The railroad car shuffled ownership
Between military and railroad companies
Eventually . . .
It was purchased by Mr. Lowry
And stored close to me
In Columbia Heights (Minnesota)
Lowry intended to refurbish the car
And send it back on tour
For all America to see
But, then he died

FUNERAL TRAIN—3

The relic somehow
Fell into the hands of a female civic group
Who got the car into touring order
Returned to former splendor
But . . .
Months before setting out
Mysteriously . . .
A prairie fire swept
Destroying this wonderful heirloom
This morning . . .
I walked the neighborhood
The internet claimed
Was the car's final site
37th and Jackson

FUNERAL TRAIN—4

At sun up, I called out the spirits
Asking them to send a sign
While noticing . . .
37th divides cracker box houses
Bad lawns and rusty cars
From bougie homes across the street
Splendid gardens, gas efficient vehicles
The space, the quiet energy
Reminded me of a Steinbeck novel
Then . . . the sun lifted
A ghost stirred, giving me a message
But . . .
That's a story for another day

Book Report—
STEALING LINCOLN'S BODY
By Thomas J. Craughwell
In the year and a half
It took Klecko
To write LINCOLNLAND
He read close to 100 books about Lincoln
Stealing Lincoln's Body . . .
Was the most entertaining
It wasn't even close
Stealing Lincoln's Body, reads like . . .
An Alfred Hitchcock film
A Quentin Tarantino film
A Werner Herzog film
Although plot points twist fast and hard
The tone is sweet
Christmas is just around the corner
This book would make a great gift

SPRINGFIELD—2

Once upon a time
In Illinois
Abraham Lincoln was dead
His body laid out, in a vault
Above ground
Somewhat unprotected
Who knew a group of hoodlums
Tried to kidnap Lincoln's corpse
Hoping to collect a ransom
The plot was foiled
But not by much
The man in charge of the cemetery
Realized at best
Security was lackluster
Later that evening
A select few dug new holes
And moved Abraham and Willie
To an undisclosed location

SPRINGFIELD—3

The well-intended grave diggers
Created an organization out of necessity
Calling themselves . . . Lincoln's Guard of Honor
They swore an oath to keep the gravesite secret
Until appropriate measures were put in place
14 years passed
Before a viable solution was offered
14 years passed
Before the Guard of Honor
Assembled a final time
To open the casket
Making certain contents were intact

SPRINGFIELD—4

13-year-old Fleetwood Lindley
Was contacted at school
Given information to make haste
And peddle his bicycle fast to the graveyard
Upon arriving, he entered a tomb
The air was rotten, it smelled of death
A coffin rested on top of two sawhorses
At that moment, he realized . . .
Why he had been called upon
It was reported Lincoln's face
Turned bronze, like a statue
Small patches of white make up
From the original burial
Glowed hauntingly
It was reported . . .
The kid, Fleetwood Lindley
Was the last human to ever see
The face of Abraham Lincoln

SPRINGFIELD—5

Down the rabbit hole I went
Read this, read that
I read a 1963 article
Published by LIFE magazine
Where Fleetwood said
He was one of the guys
Who lowered the coffin
Into the ground
While concrete was poured on top
As an extra security precaution
#Footnote—Fleetwood Lindley
Died three days after this interview
February 1st 1963

SPRINGFIELD—6

I thought about it
I marveled
I thought, and thought and thought
February 1st 1963
There was a man living on Earth
Who had seen the face of Lincoln
That was 157 days before I was born
I thought about it some more
I marveled
A fraction before I entered the world
A guy who saw Lincoln lived
I don't know why
But, this fascinated me
Enough so, that I called my publisher
Begging . . .
Does Fleetwood Lindley
Have a relative I can talk to

SPRINGFIELD—7

Presto . . .
My publisher found a son
Joe Lindley
How wonderful, he lived in Springfield
A modest sized city
Placed smack-dab, or almost
Between Chicago and St. Louis
The first question I asked was . . .
Do you follow the Cubs or Cardinals
He answered Cardinals
In a voice that suggested
There was no other answer
In a voice that possessed
A patriotic tone

SPRINGFIELD—8

Joe was cordial, Joe was kind
Decorum his ally
We discussed this, we discussed that
The moment was pleasant
After an awkward silence
He asked if I watched the HBO documentary
"Living with Lincoln"
I confessed I hadn't
He suggested I should
After alerting me
He got to do voiceovers
For his father's character

SPRINGFIELD—9

I can't tell you how much
I was enjoying talking to . . .
The son of the last living man
To see Lincoln's face
I asked Joe to throw me a bone
Tell me something random, but interesting
About Fleetwood
First answer . . .
It's a couple miles from Oakwood Cemetery
To downtown
I'm not sure how they found their way home
The night they hid Lincoln's body
There were no street lights
I don't know how they managed
But the feat in itself was impressive

SPRINGFIELD—10

Again, I asked
Tell me something random and interesting
About your father Fleetwood
Something you haven't thought to tell
To any other reporter
Second answer . . .
Pause . . .
Pause . . .
Something, my favorite thing or memory . . .
My parents, their bodies
Are buried almost on the exact spot
Where Lincoln's body was stashed
The first night they reburied him

SPRINGFIELD—11

And with that golden nugget
I said thank you and goodnight
What a thrill, what a thrill
To talk with a decent man
Who fully realized
How fortunate he was
To be of the bloodline
That kept Lincoln safe

BIRD & VERANDA—1

It was still too cold to read on the veranda
But I did, I reread WELCOME TO AMERICA
By Linda Boström Knausgård
I don't usually reread books
But the protagonist was a selective mute
The book made me smile
It reminded me, of me
How I was pressured to acclimate
A bird popped out of the shrubs
Landed at my feet and barked
A truculent cuss, no bigger than a canary
I'd never seen this species
The body was black, or blue
Depending on the angle
Its head was covered with a brown hood
I snapped several photos
The bird didn't flinch
It moved close, it barked
I posted the image on Facebook
And asked for help identifying
My new favorite bird

BIRD & VERANDA—2

Brown-Headed Cowbird

- They prefer fields and spaces
  Large enough to keep livestock
- Females lay 40 eggs a season
- They don't build nests
- They dump their eggs into nests
  Of other birds
  At the expense of the host chicks
- 220 species of birds
  Have been documented
  Raising brown-headed cowbirds unknowingly
- Young cowbirds develop faster
  Then nest mates, who oftentimes
  Get tossed out or smothered
- In winter, brown-headed cowbirds
  Have joined roosts with blackbirds
  Containing as many as
  Five million birds

KATO—1

Half my age, twice as smart
The librarian joined me on the veranda
Sipping cocktails, discussing books
Pounding cocktails, discussing books
She asked what I was reading . . .
THE LYNCHINGS IN DULUTH
By Michael Fedo
I mentioned it moved quick
I mentioned . . .
It was Minnesota's saddest moment
The librarian reminded me
Sad isn't a competition
Sad is sad
Then she asked if I was aware
That the nation's largest mass execution
Took place 90 minutes away
I answered . . . no, she continued
In Mankato, day after Christmas
38 Native Americans were hung
The order of execution
Was given by no other
Than President Abraham Lincoln

KATO—2

I went in, I came out
Fresh cocktails in each hand
The librarian handed me a list of books
Splendid cursive, on the back of an envelope
LINCOLN AND THE INDIANS
David A. Nichols
38 NOOSES
Scott W. Berg
THROUGH DAKOTA EYES
Gary Clayton Anderson & Alan R. Woolworth
THE RELENTLESS BUSINESS OF TREATIES
Martin Case
SAVAGE CONVERSATIONS
Leanne Howe
DAKOTA PRISONER OF WAR LETTERS
Clifford Canku & Michael Simon
A couple thousand pages
Passed like melted butter
Who knew . . . who knew
These topics were never taught
To white kids, growing up in the suburbs

KATO—3

As I entered the parking lot
It hit me like a sledgehammer
I was wearing plaid shorts
I used to wear plaid shorts
To be ironic
But now I wear plaid shorts
Because I am an old man
Next, I noticed my road-trip provisions
Consisted of a gallon of water
And an orange
It was two hours before sunrise
It was quiet, I was alone, I wondered
If ever in history
A young man headed toward adventure
With a jug of water and an orange
My heart sunk
As I engaged the ignition
And pulled out of the parking lot
Not certain how to proceed

KATO—4

Without invitation
I pulled into Mankato, sat in the dark
Alone, on sacred ground
I didn't know the protocol, it was dark
Ill prepared, ill equipped
I waited for sunrise
To attempt contact with the spirits
Orange, pink, yellow
The sun bounced, the town remained empty
I assumed the park would be huge
Huge enough to symbolize a city's attempt
To mask shame that should never fade
But, the site was small
Tiny
Mentally, I hadn't prepared for this
As I unbuckled my seatbelt
I questioned my place
My purpose in this continuing saga
I got out of my car
And walked toward the white buffalo

KATO—5

Even though I believe
I feel stupid when I say . . .
Spirits, give me a sign
Which, is exactly what I said
Staring into the eyes
Of the great white buffalo
67 tons of Kasota limestone
Which the placard informed me
Represented heritage
And survival
Of the Dakota people
Even though I believe
I get embarrassed
When I say it
But, I said it
And meant it with all my heart
Spirits, give me a sign

I stared at the buffalo, I stared at the buffalo
I stared at the buffalo
Not knowing what to think
Not knowing what to expect
I stared at the buffalo
I stared straight into his eyes
No more than 90 seconds passed
Before I heard, felt a thwap
On my collarbone
As if somebody flicked me
My mind raced fast enough
That logic zipped past fear
I turned around
Nobody was there
Slowly, I looked at my collarbone
The part that got thwapped
Exhibit "A" indicated . . .
A bird shit on me
Immediately I understood
It was all too clear, I felt sad
But understood
My concern was unwanted
So, I returned home

EASTERN TERMINUS—1

Who knew . . .
Lincoln owned several parcels of land
In Iowa
He never visited these properties
But, he did go to Council Bluffs
To talk to a smart guy
A guy who would help him
Connect the nation's coasts
With a transcontinental railroad
Who knew . . .
The good people of Council Bluffs
Would one day place an obelisk
On the bluff
On the very spot Lincoln stood
So people like us could visit
To stand in his footsteps
I didn't know this
But when I did
I began making preparations

EASTERN TERMINUS—2

At work, I asked the guy who mixed bread . . .
Didn't you do a quarter of college
In Council Bluffs
He smiled, he replied . . .
Part of a quarter
I asked . . .
Did you ever go to Lincoln Park
Did you ever see the obelisk
He smiled, he replied . . .
Yeah, I saw it
The park should be called
Crackhead park
But for the most part
Everyone gets along there

EASTERN TERMINUS—3

The plan, St. Paul to Omaha
Pick up my grandson Monster
Turn around, back to Iowa
To see if we can find Lincoln's ghost
While lurking around his holy obelisk
From past experience
I have discovered
Adventure tends to magnify
About the time vampires go to sleep
I grabbed an orange
And a jug of water
Beginning my journey
On streets that remained empty

EASTERN TERMINUS—4

I pick Iowa, over the ocean
Iowa, over the mountains
Iowa, over LA, DC or Hawaii
Every time I drive across the Hawkeye state
A curiosity occurs
Did I live here in a previous life
Is there a chance
I could close shop on the prairie
I've felt an energy of belonging
But my mind's-eye can't get a visual
Clear Lake came close . . . but
Decorah and DeSoto too . . . but
Every time I pulled out of these towns
I realized
These pursuits were nothing more
Than another spent dream

Crossing the prairie
It's easy to get lonely
But, on this day, it wasn't that
I felt uncertain
About what, I'm not sure
It doesn't matter
The spell was broken
The moment I came upon the wind farm
There wasn't a convenient place to park
But I did . . .
Turbines . . . HUGE
Big enough to be God's pets
Then I felt bad because . . .
Lately I hadn't paid attention to God
I felt ashamed
As I hopped back into my car
Wondering how and why
I had let the world get between us

EASTERN TERMINUS—6

Many years ago, or probably longer
I read Bukowski's poem, "Nirvana"
I liked it, claimed it as a favorite
I read it to whoever would listen
They liked it, for various reasons
I liked it, because . . .
The poem hints
Each of us has a personal paradise
Bukowski's was in North Carolina
In a café
I on the other hand . . .
Had gone over half a century
Cut loose from purpose
Who would have guessed
Who would have guessed
Nirvana could surface in Iowa
It was hard to stop smiling

EASTERN TERMINUS—7

Paradise and clarity
Intersect at 4:52 AM
During a random stop, random moment
Parked in the lot of the Kum & Go
Across the street
The Adair Budget Inn
Circumstance complicates, but . . .
I could see myself living here
Everyday
There is a brief moment
Minutes before sunrise
When birds come together
To mount their dawn chorus
It's during this moment
I remember, I consider
Kevin Costner might be wrong
Iowa might be heaven
In that case, that would make Adair
The happiest town on Earth

EASTERN TERMINUS—8

Jesus on the cross became a thing
After I drove across three states
Pulled into Nebraska
Had a couple of highballs
Jesus on the cross was created for
Grandchildren who loiter around Golgotha
Grandchildren who set Barabbas free
Grandchildren who don't refresh my highball
Jesus on the cross is best achieved
By placing thumbs into tiny palms
Pressing on tendons
Lifting, swinging, till eyes roll backwards
Jesus on the cross incites screaming, laughter
High pitch responses
None of which are sanctioned
By my daughter or son-in-law
However, the ritual is trending
In addition to my grandchildren
Friends, neighbors and cousins
Clamor to join my clientele
With each ensuing visit

In the corn
I was technician, Monster the pilot
Wind pulled hard, lifting him tiptoed
He smiled, he asked
Is the kite closer to us or God
I didn't know, so I told the truth
Halfway to heaven, a mile from Moses
Time passed, comfortable in silence
I recalled visiting a fortune teller
She explained . . .
Your exploits have drawn you acclaim
Enjoy them if you wish
But, know their results
Didn't manifest for you
That energy will pass to a grandson
As Monster reeled in the kite
I wanted to share our connection
But, he was too young to understand
And if my daughter found out . . .
Even though Monster was ignorant of his destiny
All was fine, he asked for ice cream
Halfway to heaven, a mile from Moses

EASTERN TERMINUS—10

After the corn
Monster and I worked on his A-B-C's
Actually, the ABC part was fine
The real trouble started around
L-M-N-O-P
Eventually he got it, and when he did
I suggested he should take a nap
So he would have ample energy
When we went to Council Bluffs
To look for Lincoln's ghost
His mood became dark
Eyes fogged over
Until a smirk developed
Until he issued a counter proposal
G-Pa, I could take a nap
But if I did
I wouldn't have time to show you
George Washington's secret grave
How could I resist

EASTERN TERMINUS—11

Back in the corn
93 degrees, no cloud cover
Twisting–Turning
Left–Right
Forward–Back
Bugs head level
Bugs in my eyes
Huffing–Puffing
Soaked with sweat
Then it happened
He turned around, faced me
A curious look
A look of defeat
Tears rolled down his cheek
G-Pa, I can't find it
But I promise
George Washington's grave
It's really close
Then he wailed
I had to smile
Monster believed his own fable
I have never been more proud

EASTERN TERMINUS—12

They call it a bluff
But it's taller than a bluff
Just short of a tiny mountain
A narrow road spirals upward
At an impossible angle
When you finally reach the obelisk
There's nowhere to park
Nowhere to pull over
You simply have to stop
At the monument
Another road intersects
At a 90-degree angle
Stretching all the way out
To Lincoln Park
Each side is lined with mansions
Half a century older than mine
I killed the ignition
I gave a nod to Monster
Indicating show time starts in 3–2–1

EASTERN TERMINUS—13

58,738 days have passed
Since Lincoln stood on this spot
Staring across a state line
Into Omaha
58,738 days have passed
Since Lincoln dared to consider
Connecting the coasts, not knowing
This was as far west as he would get
58,738 days have passed
Gosh, I hope there's a way
For him to know
I remember
But if there isn't, it doesn't matter
I'm connecting legacies with Monster
The win is ours

EASTERN TERMINUS—14

I tell Monster
Place your hands on the obelisk
Close your eyes
Concentrate, feel the energy
Let's look for Lincoln's ghost
We proceed
Minutes later, I open my eyes
Monster is gone, I panic
Until I notice him
Sitting on a reverence bench
Made of designer stone
Sitting next to two old pensioners
Monster's playing a video game
I express disappointment
His eyes never leave the screen
As he explained . . .
Keep trying G-Pa
But I got a message
Lincoln is gone for the day

SNOW OWL

A bank of treadmills, each occupied
I have to pee
Upon my return, the gym is empty
Weird, scary, rapture . . . I wasn't sure
So I peeked outside, people faced me
Heads tilted back, staring toward the sun
I joined them, Hark . . . an owl
A snow owl, huge, perched on top of the strip mall
Bigger than I might have imagined
If I took time to consider owls
But I don't like them, I don't know why
Kinda like people from New Jersey
We stare, and stare, and stare, and . . .
A woman not much bigger than the owl
Says . . . Fuck, it's gorgeous
Then she blushed and apologized
For her offensive language
To which the man with broad shoulders replied
I'm pretty sure that word was invented
For moments just like this

TAVERN ON GRAND

The ship seems to start sinking
Just around midnight
About the time my tumbler drains empty
Business is slow, so . . .
Barkeep suggests last call
Which automatically makes me want another
But, I've already closed out my tab . . .
Twice
Not that anyone cares, but . . .
It's never good form to broadcast indecision
A woman across the bar stares at me
Then she stares at me some more
Before announcing . . .
She's aware, booze hasn't made me happy
I flinched as she continued . . .
Overcast skies won't do
Birds sing louder, when singing into sunshine
I wasn't sure what that meant
All I could do was shrug, knowing
The ship seems to start sinking
Every time I allow
Alcohol and conversation
To share the same space

JAYHAWK—1

Other than Christ
More books have been written about Lincoln
Than anybody else
I bought the newest one . . .
LINCOLN ON THE VERGE
It starts with Lincoln
Going to Troy, Kansas
A year before the election
In the middle of December
The weather was freezing
He rode in an open carriage
Some guy wrapped him
In some kind of bear-bison pelt
Still . . . Lincoln turned blue
Eventually, he thawed
And spoke to 40 citizens
For close to two hours
Mostly about abolishing slavery
The book said . . . the meeting hall remained
That's when I asked her . . .
Wanna go to Kansas
To look for Lincoln's ghost

JAYHAWK—2

Drive through heat, drive through glare
Drive–Drive–Drive
Past prairies, past plains
Once you exit Iowa
Everything becomes still
Pilgrims and roadkill
Drive–Drive–Drive
Weather woman says . . .
Heat index feels like 107
We won't be deterred, because
For all the times I said . . .
Baby, you aren't in Kansas anymore
You finally are
You made it
Welcome to the Jayhawk state
Welcome to Troy

We didn't want to come off big city
We didn't want to appear Hollywood
So we left our Ray-Bans in the car
Big mistake, Troy was bright
What once glared was now blinding
The town was brick, we baked
The town was empty, sweat flowed
The state flag appeared unapologetic
Exercising minimal effort
Hanging limp against the pole
40 minutes passed, not a soul stepped forward
City Hall—Closed, Courthouse—Closed
Library—Masonic Hall—Saloon—Closed
She looked tired, thirsty, soggy
She looked like a bomb, about to explode

JAYHAWK—4

For a town the size of a thimble
It's amazing it took us . . .
A million hours to find the Lincoln monument
Eventually, after stumbling into a cranny
I caught her rolling her eyes
Underwhelmed
Her voice remained silent
But her face conveyed an expression
Insinuating . . .
We did all this, for that
I studied the Lincoln bust
I studied the lecture hall
I was at peace
But I didn't feel Lincoln's energy
I couldn't make a connection
I was curious if my muse did
But, trying to obtain that result
Might be like . . .
Throwing a match into a gas can
But me being me, I couldn't help myself
I had to ask

JAYHAWK—5

She said . . .
Before I answer about Lincoln
Have you ever seen the movie
"Children of the Corn"
Or one of a million movies
Where an unsuspecting couple
Enters the empty town
But actually it isn't empty
It's filled with devil worshippers
Who wait patiently for sundown
Who wait patiently to sacrifice fools
We stood, we stared
She smiled, kinda, before pointing out
I haven't seen anyone, not a soul
For the briefest moment
I didn't know what to do
But then a man appeared
I considered it must be an angel, until
I noticed he wore mint green eyewear
And lisped like Truman Capote
As things turned out . . .
Dude was just a dude

JAYHAWK—6

The man with mint green eyewear
Inched closer, yet kept distant
To be honest, he creeped me out
Deadpan giggles
And an orchestrated lisp
Delivered at an octave
Created to cause discomfort
Worse than that . . .
Was the glare he delivered
With eyes like those found
On plastic doll heads
I didn't want to ask
Where the closest motel was
But saw no other option
He asked which way we were going
I said we were staying
Here, in Troy
He shook his head slowly . . .
There's no place to stay
You might find something
In 30 or 40 miles

MIZZOU—1

She rode shot gun
Perched on a powder keg
Fuse, down to the nub
Lucky for me, lucky for us
Everything . . .
This, that and the other
Was void of spark
Before I could ask
She fulfilled destiny
She fulfilled destiny, by . . .
Pointing a finger
And offering verbal commands
Until . . .
We crossed the state line
Leaving Kansas . . .
In our rearview mirror

MIZZOU—2

The sign announced it
She read it
I repeated . . .
St. Joseph
She said she heard of it
I agreed
But neither of us
Remembered attributes
That might sway
Our opinion of this city
One way or another

Not wanting to be at a disadvantage
She employed Google
St. Joseph was . . .
Gateway to the west
Where Jesse James was shot
Home to the Pony Express
Birthplace to . . .
Walter Cronkite
Jane Wyman
Hip Hop artist . . .
Eminem
National Council for Home and Safety
Reported St. Joseph
Was more dangerous than . . .
Ferguson
St. Louis
And Kansas City

MIZZOU—4

Fredrick Avenue is like . . .
A heavyweight champion
Who wouldn't quit with enough ability
To defend safety and reputation
JAB–JAB
I got the sense
This place used to be special
Important
JAB–JAB
Broken glass, plastic bottles
Rusty bumpers, orphaned hubcaps
Forgotten . . . lethargic
JAB–JAB
Up ahead, she spots a Ferris wheel
In the parking lot of JCPenney
She says it's good luck
She says we should stay
JAB–JAB
Sucker punch and 8-9-10
Down for the count

Room 215, chock full of amenities
Sliding door, balcony
Curtains thick as a tapestry
Ice machine in the courtyard
I liked the place
It had grit
The kind of place a bad guy
From a Cormac McCarthy novel
Would kill or be killed
She looked dead
Stretched out across the bed
Stretched out motionless
In a position that suggested nap
I knew better
She would stay down until morning
Which gave me permission
To grab my flight bag
Exit . . .
And look for a suitable launch pad

MIZZOU—6

I saw an abandoned water park
A big space
Big enough to support a stadium
From the look of things
It might have been vacant for a decade
If not . . .
Long enough for chain-link to rust
Long enough for shrubs to break through asphalt
Long enough for 1000 sumps
To pockmark the terrain
Gosh it was hot, I was already soaked
Gosh I was thirsty, I opened my bag
And pulled out my kite
There was some wind
Not a lot, but maybe enough
I wasn't sure
Gosh it was hot

The kite was up, barely
I wondered if the wind would increase
I wondered who was approaching me
In so many words
I was joined by two homeless panhandlers
The one on my left was blond and old
The one on his left was gray and older
Like me, they were soaked
Like me, they watched the kite
Bobbing for its life
I asked . . .
Where can a guy buy booze around here
Older pointed catty-corner
At the Phillips 66
I said, no . . . not beer
I want hard stuff
Older clarified
They sell whiskey or vodka
What else would you want

MIZZOU—8

I laughed and explained
Where I live, you can't buy booze
At a gas station
This news appeared
To genuinely upset my new friends
I asked a favor
I don't want to reel in the kite, so . . .
If I buy you guys a bottle
Will you bring me back a liter
Of whiskey
Their eyes announced JACKPOT
Their hands received $60
Without a word
They disappeared

The sun showed no mercy
The kite limped along
My mind was empty, on cruise control
Or maybe I was thinking of Cleveland
When Old and Older returned
With plastic bags
And schoolboy grins
Voila . . .
A bottle of Jack Daniels for them
A bottle of Jack Daniels for me
They offered change
I offered confusion, and a wink
What, no Micks in this town
Where's the Jameson
Older shrugged and said . . .
I hope you're joking
Cuz if not, just remember
We could have got Seagram's 7
Within moments
The bottles were tilted

MIZZOU—10

Stooped and deflated
We baked on the asphalt
From the look in my friends' eyes
I could tell we were in agreement
Few things detoured heat
But . . . whiskey was one of them
The moment shifted
I spaced off
My thoughts were with the kite
When I came back
I noticed Older, the more he looked up
The more he smiled
I passed him the string
He accepted

Not long after, as if scripted
A gust emerged, the kite climbed
I was drunk, I was happy
Older maneuvered the rig
With . . .
An extended smile and shaky hands
What could be said . . .
When the quiet calls
It's easy to get details
I did
I saw a tear slide down Older's cheek
He saw me witness this and explained
I used to fly kites
Back on a farm in Oklahoma
Then he handed back the line
And my new friends exited
As quiet as they entered
I capped my bottle
And packed my gear
Feeling somber
As I made my way to the Ferris wheel

TWO GEESE

They're back, honking
Bringing joy, at least to me
They're back, searching for food
The dumpster is empty
I toss them milk buns
The oven man indicates my gesture
Is an open invitation to trouble
The pleasure was mine . . .
How natural they seem
Relaxed in their stance
Waiting, for nothing to happen
Our shift is over
One by one, bakers drive away
Until, I am left alone, in my car
Staring at two geese
Taking mental note of a nobility
Difficult for humans to decipher
Silence, time passes, nobody moves
I set my gaze and let it sink in
Knowing eventually
I will forget them
Like everything else

A MOMENT OF HAPPY

In the corner of the parking lot
Behind the steering wheel of a Jetta
I relaxed, in a trance
Reading ZORBA THE GREEK
A copy mother gifted me
I'd read GREEK PASSION
And LAST TEMPTATION OF CHRIST
But, she assured me, this was better
A house finch, perched on my wing mirror
He chirped happy, we stared at each other
Joy filled my heart, at a record clip
I considered contact, but the window was up
Perhaps the house finch read my mind
Immediately he flew to the window
Pecked my finger pressed against the glass
Then bounced back to the wing mirror
Where he said goodbye in finch
Before ascending upward
And the sky was no longer empty

SPILLVILLE—1

What a wonder, what a world
She applied make-up
Listened to music
I was never a fan of classical
She was
I didn't listen to . . .
National Public Radio
She did
Man on the airwaves
Advised us to stay tuned
In a moment, he would return
To tell us how a scarlet tanager
Helped a Czechoslovakian composer
Create a legacy work in Iowa
She turned off the light
Announcing it was time to leave
I like Czechs
I like birds
Tick–Tock, I settled in
What a wonder
What a world

SPILLVILLE—2

The man on the airwaves said . . .
In 1893 Czech composer
Antonin Dvorák traveled . . .
Europe to New York for money
New York to Iowa for vacation
In pursuit of a town . . .
Spillville
Home to Czechs, clockmakers
And the scarlet tanager
Curiosity peaked
I turned down the volume
Dug through the book crate
Presto . . .
I found it

SPILLVILLE—3

My mother the Mystic
Gave me a book
She had since 1956
A GOLDEN GUIDE TO BIRDS
129 full-colored pictures
Every page dog-eared
Weathered . . .
I didn't know
What a scarlet tanager looked like
Until page 111
My goodness, so gorgeous
The description was spot on
It said . . .
Identification of this
Unmistakable bird is obvious
Tick–Tock, summer was waning
Time kills deals
Spillville or bust

SPILLVILLE—4

After crossing the state line
After waving to the Amish
I drove forward
I thought back
To growing up Polish
I was taught
Keep Czechs at a distance
That is until . . .
Germans or Russians entered
On those occasions
Slavic blood forms an alliance
Due to shared wiring and sensibilities
Czechs aren't bad people
Just quiet
A trait difficult
For a Pole to understand

SPILLVILLE—5

Tick–Tock, down the hill
Bily Clocks in Spillville
Iowa's gem, America's gem
Two brothers, farmers
Two brothers, bachelors
Two brothers who . . .
Stayed put, excelled
And never went beyond
35 miles from home
Ever
I asked my guide Shirley
How this could be
She shrugged
Saying . . .
It wasn't uncommon
For these times
For these people

SPILLVILLE—6

Shirley started the tour
At the statuary clock
Almost ten feet tall
Carved from black walnut
Oak and boxwood
Inside . . .
Stood countless figurines
Lincoln, Shakespeare
Antonin Dvorák
Ulysses S. Grant
The Roosevelts
Teddy and FDR
Other carvings included . . .
Civic leaders
Neighbors
Even the postmaster
I mentioned
A Pole would have included
Their village bartender
Shirley shrugged

The American Pioneer History clock
Took four years to construct
57 panels of American history
Over eight feet tall
Over 500 pounds
The Bily brothers agreed
This was their legacy
European cherrywood
And walnut were enough
To entice Henry Ford
To visit Iowa
To take a look
Tick–Tock, Mr. Ford thought
This must be obtained
And displayed at the World's Fair
Tick–Tock, Mr. Ford thought
And threw out a number
One million dollars
The Bily brothers explained
They already had money
But only one favorite clock
Tick–Tock, what a shock
Henry Ford left . . . disappointed

SPILLVILLE—8

Intoxicating
The ticking, the tocking
Chimes and calliopes
Shirley's kindness
Zucchini bread recipes
I explained
I was off to pursue
A scarlet tanager
When I asked for advice
Shrugging was a thing of the past
My guide straightened up
And informed me with certainty
You should go . . .
To the World's Smallest Church

SPILLVILLE—9

I asked Shirley, how far was it . . .
To the World's Smallest Church
She answered . . .
A spell
I wasn't sure how far a spell was
My GPS said 11 miles
Barely cracking double digits
Might indicate . . .
My destination was nigh
It was, but it wasn't
Forget the gravel
And maze-like conditions
Driving through corn
Tall enough to blot out the sun
For a moment
I became overwhelmed
I was alone in Iowa
And I honestly didn't know
If I should be happy or sad
Amidst this corn odyssey

FESTINA—1

About a quarter-mile away
I spotted a belfry
And began to experience
The best kind of anxious
But, I had to keep focus
I had to slow down
A sign alerted me
Narrow bridge ahead
The very moment
And I mean, the very moment
I tamped down my attention
Whoosh—
A scarlet tanager
Zipped across my sightline
Left to right, perfectly level
Gosh that was pleasant
An objective met
Without breaking a sweat
Few things are better
Than fish jumping
Into the boat

FESTINA—2

Pulling into the parking lot
I was so pleased
I didn't know what to do
An appropriate song wasn't apparent
So I had to improvise . . .
Hark the herald
Angels sing
Call me Klecko
The new corn king
I liked the song
A lot
And repeated it softly
About a million times

FESTINA—3

Behind the World's Smallest Church
Exists a makeshift graveyard
Toward the back
I saw crows and grackles
I began to feel embarrassed
I can't differentiate species
The moment turned morose
So, I shifted thought
To Robert Bly's poem "The Grackles"
Because my memory seldom floats
I plugged into a paraphrased version
Only found in my mental warehouse
"Grackles stroll across sorrow
Their toes have spring
When they walk over footprints
The dreamer made last night"
I wondered, who was the last dreamer
To visit the World's Smallest Church
I went to look for footprints
My smile returned

FESTINA—4

Markers and tombstones
Nestled flush against the corn break
It was quiet, but not lonely
Soft sounds came forward
How could I know, but I did
The dead were communicating joy
In particular Johann Gartner
A guy whose tombstone read . . .
FOUGHT WITH NAPOLEON BONAPARTE
AT MOSCOW AND WATERLOO
I stood with him
Longer than intended
And began to feel
My departure would mean betrayal
Uncertain of protocol
I committed audibly
To adopting his soul
And gave every assurance
I'd return Christmas Day

CLERMONT—1

Around the bar
The topic shifts
To my post-pandemic hair
The bounty of its yield
I mentioned, I was shooting
For a Kurt Cobain bob
She, nodded with uncertainty
Before suggesting
Keep it David Lynch length
He has great hair
Around the bar
The topic shifts
To ERASERHEAD
TWIN PEAKS
BLUE VELVET
I became bored
I wanted to discuss . . .
THE STRAIGHT STORY
A film . . . None of my companions
Were familiar with

CLERMONT—2

Around the bar
I explained to patrons
The Lynch films they discussed
Were merely disciples
But . . . THE STRAIGHT STORY
It was the messiah
A masterpiece
The old man . . .
The John Deere lawnmower
Simplicity, truth, kindness
I wished I was there
But . . . I was drunk
And couldn't remember
Where "there" was
So, I texted my publisher
And asked if she knew
She knows a lot

CLERMONT—3

A text was returned, announcing . . .
CLERMONT—IOWA
P.S. They have a Lincoln Park
With a statue for its namesake
It's over 100 years old
Made by Bissell
He put another Lincoln statue
In Edinburgh
He likes to build them tall
Hard to photograph
Unless you get there in the morning

CLERMONT—4

Walk the circle
Lincoln Park, sunrise
Walk the circle
Surrounding monuments
Surrounding Lincoln
Footsteps form a pattern
A pattern forms a rhythm
It seems as if a sound
Should accompany the motion
Something splendid
Something melodic
But alas, sound is empty
But, empty isn't bad
When it's small town silence
Walk the circle

Perhaps it was the circular motion
That put me in sync with the cosmos
Or, maybe it was grace
Either way . . .
I saw him, I saw Lincoln's ghost
Leaning on a park bench
Straining forward
Eyes focused on Main Street
With a look that suggested
He didn't know what he was looking for
But, there was a grin
Soft and serious
Which seemed to indicate
He would accept
Anything that came his way

CLERMONT—6

Downshifting, hydraulic brakes
An oil-tanker semi trolls past
Lincoln's mouth forms a dumb grin
I knew what he was wondering
I almost blurted out
She holds 10,000 gallons
The "almost" jinxed the moment
Lincoln vanished
The sun was up, I sat down
My vision blurred, it's hard to describe
I was overwhelmed by yellow
Filled by yellow
Not the yellow associated with cowardice
I don't know what yellow was
But it was yellow
And my body contained joy
More joy than I could process

CLERMONT—7

Churchill was buck-naked
When he noticed the ghost of Lincoln
Wilhelmina, Queen of the Netherlands
Saw the ghost and fainted
First Lady Coolidge saw him
Eisenhower saw him
Lady Bird Johnson, Truman too
They went on record
Most of them bragged
They had seen the ghost of Lincoln
Maureen Reagan spotted Lincoln
Standing in her chamber
Wearing a red robe
In the morning, she mentioned this
To her father Ronald
Who returned the admission
With a frown before advising
Next time, send him my way
I have a couple of problems
He might be able to help me with

CLERMONT—8

Exiting Clermont
My mind was blank
I don't think I was trying to think
But, I thought
When you are bourgeois
You can tell the world
You can tell the media
That you saw Lincoln's ghost
But, if you are a bread baker
And announce you saw Lincoln's ghost
It will only stir the pot
And cause problems

BILL—1

Dear Mr. Murray,
My name is Julie Pfitzinger
Of Paris Morning Publications
One of my authors, Klecko
Is a 40-year Master bread baker
And poet
In June, he won the 2020
Midwest Book Award
I've been working with Klecko
For some time, but I never heard
Why he decided to become a baker
When I asked, he was quick to answer
It appears that you, Mr. Murray
Played an integral part
In Klecko's life-changing decision
I thought you'd like to know
Best wishes,
Julie

BILL—2

Hello Bill,
As a young man, I felt like a loser
My friends and family graduated college
I baked bread
Then I saw . . . THE RAZOR'S EDGE
When closing credits rolled
For the first time, I believed
I could have impact
If I baked sourdough
And read books
Somerset Maugham . . .
His Larry Darrell was soft
But your version
Was who I wanted to be
I have had the best life
It would have never happened
Without your contribution
If I knew how to pay you back
I would, but I don't
Thank you seems weak
But it's all I got
Thanks . . .
Klecko

LEIF ENGER—1

The tavern was quiet, my publisher smiled
With a look indicating
She had news of the world
The tavern was quiet, until she announced
HITMAN-BAKER-CASKETMAKER
Had been nominated
For a Midwest Book Award
My publisher smiled, asking if I realized
Opportunities would multiply
If we won, I could write my own ticket
The tavern was quiet, my publisher smiled
Asking, if you win, when you win
How will you use your momentum
I considered the question
For nearly 3o seconds, before asking
Have you read VIRGIL WANDER
She nodded yes, to which I responded
I want to fly kites, with the author
Can you make that happen
The tavern was quiet, my publisher smiled

"It was the greatest day
Of my life
Flying kites with Leif Enger
On Lake Superior
Gosh . . .
It was kinda like
Taking batting practice
With Babe Ruth
In Yankee Stadium"

—Klecko

LEIF ENGER—3

On flight day, on the dune
It was colder than anticipated
Because my host was thoughtful
We had everything
Caramel pecan rolls
A thermos of coffee
A delightful conversation
About the time young Leif Enger
Set out to break a world record
Set out to keep his kite afloat
For 57 hours, in the dead of winter
On Lake Osakis
The attempt lasted 39 hours
Long enough to make him smile
Years after
Finally, he announced
Time to put kites in the sky
The scene was set, picture perfect
The moment qualified for paradise
Except . . .
There was no wind

No wind, Leif smiles
Crash go the waves, splash goes the water
I stand, disappointed
My parafoil grounded
No wind, Leif smiles
Projecting certainty, while assembling
A French Military kite
He speaks of
Chinese kites that need no wind
How it's possible to fly them
In gymnasiums or warehouses
He speaks of
Spirit Man kites
Made in an English loft
Moments after, the French Military kite
Is assembled . . . WHOOSH
300, 400, 500 feet
The only kite in the sky
Which makes it so special
When my friend handed it to me

DULUTH—1

When you go to Hawk Ridge
If you don't see hawks
There's always hawk people
I saw no hawks at Hawk Ridge
I saw women layered in thermal
She, said to Her
There's lots of vampires in Canal Park
When Her spotted me
Watching Her and She
Her asked my opinion
About the Duluth populace
Hmmm . . . I wondered
Hmmm . . . I answered
They are Minnesota's San Francisco
Minnesota's Seattle
She looked at Her
Before looking to me and explaining
Makes sense
Vampires require large bodies of water
I didn't know that
NOTE TO SELF . . .

DULUTH—2

Gull here, gulls there
I pay them notice
They pay me a mindful eye
Because I was alone, I was brave
I talked to them
Telepathically
I said . . .
Beg your pardon
I was under the impression
Your species was generic
Akin to pigeons, doves with grit
The gulls remained silent, I continued
Nah . . . you aren't generic
You're badass
Would it be accurate to say
Gulls are . . .
The French Foreign Legion of birds
The colony circled
The gulls answered
KA-KAW
And with that, all was merry

DULUTH—3

She urged
Let's go to Park Point
Key West of the Midwest
Let's gather rocks
Fill the knapsack
Lug them into town
Go to the antique store
Purchase a receptacle
Even though we don't understand
The difference between a rock and an agate
We'll bring them home
And fill our home
With memories and wonder
And maybe, if we're lucky
One of the rocks
Might contain a ghost
From the Edmund Fitzgerald

JONATHAN FRANZEN—1

God created birds
Adam assigned their names
Saint Francis . . .
Loved them with all his heart
Jonathan Franzen . . .
Loved them more

JONATHAN FRANZEN—2

Dear Ms. Pfitzinger
Thanks for passing on Klecko's note
And questions
I love a publisher
Who looks after her authors
And Klecko sounds great
Below is my reply to him

Warm regards,
Jon F.

To the Baker,
Many thanks for your note
I have to start by disagreeing with you
Being a "lister" is many things
But, you're the first person I know
Who's ever called it cool
Coolness is in the eye of the beholder
And I am afraid you are vastly outnumbered
But, I'm always happy to hear from someone
Who pays attention to birds
Especially from someone
Who pays enough attention
To have a wish list

JONATHAN FRANZEN—4

Congrats on finding a scarlet tanager
I remember seeing one myself
In Minnesota, a brilliant red male
In a state park, not far south
Of the Twin Cities
My friend and I also saw
Red-headed woodpeckers there
If you haven't seen one of those
I have a new suggestion for your wish list

JONATHAN FRANZEN—5

The quiet way
In which seeing a bird
Can change your life . . .
I hear you

JONATHAN FRANZEN—6

To your questions . . .

JONATHAN FRANZEN—7

#1—I've seen quite a few scarlet tanagers
Including a good dozen of them
In Central Park in New York
But, I will never see enough of them
In the intensity of their color
They seem to me
They most tropical of U.S. birds
And indeed
They are tropical
Eight months out of twelve

#2—My life at this point, runs on two tracks
One consisting of experiences of birds
The other of everything else
So it's hard to single out
A sighting that clearly stands above
A hundred others
If you made me name one anyway
I might mention . . .
Those great hornbills I saw in India
And wrote about briefly in . . .
WHY BIRDS MATTER
It's one of the few times in my life
When I literally found myself
Crying out with joy

JONATHAN FRANZEN—9

I love birding in Minnesota
And it would be great
To hang out with the baker
Next time I'm there
Thanks for the invitation

The Birder

DEAR DIARY

Euan Kerr is an MPR reporter
He is Scottish, he is kind
Today, he posted photos on Facebook
From the State Fair grounds
Of a museum of Cedar Waxwings
Bouncing about a tree, happy
As if they surrounded Bambi
Fact, they are kind
They eat in shifts, nobody budges
Realizing patience is a virtue
When Brown-Headed Cowbirds
Hatch from eggs
Dropped in a waxwings nest
The crow offspring will likely perish
They can't survive
On the waxwings' fruit diet
NOTE TO SELF . . .
The meek are inheriting the Earth

BEHIND THE MANSION—1

Avoiding annoyances and bustle
In a parking lot, from my car, I dialed
She picked up, sounded medicated
Me—It's been 40 years, huh
I heard you were dying so I called
Her—I'm almost dead, talk fast
Me—Wanna hear a secret
Her—Yeah
Me—When you babysat me, I loved you
Her—I know
Me—When I got older, at baseball practice
We discussed babysitters we wanted to bang
I chose you
Her—Over Katie Olsen
Me—Yep
Her—Thanks for picking me
Katie was a whore (pause)
It's starting to hurt, hold on a second . . .
The conversation detoured
Shallow breaths, quiet continued
And more of the same

BEHIND THE MANSION—2

Was she asleep, I wasn't sure
Was she . . . I didn't know what to do
I didn't know, time passed
Tick–Tock, what to do
I heard a gurgle, I heard hello
The conversation resumed
Me—You traveled a lot, huh
Her—I got around
Me—Like a hundred countries
Her—Close, but never Italy
I'll never get there now
God Damn it, how did that happen
Me—I've never been there
Her—But you have time
Me—I can't, I pledged an oath
Her—Huh . . .
Me—I swore to God, if you don't go
I don't go, it's a blood oath
Fuck Italy
Her—You must go
Me—Fuck Italy
Her—I love you Danny

Dear Diary . . .
I Googled best books about pandemic stories
Down the rabbit hole I went
Zooming past lists compiled by
The New York Times, Goodreads
Vulture and Book Riot
I saw selections from faculty
At Harvard, Yale and Columbia
Sure . . . they had THE PLAGUE
By Albert Camus
Sure . . . they had THE STAND
By Stephen King
But, nobody had
MOONSTONE:
THE BOY WHO NEVER WAS
By Sjón
Not only is it the best pandemic book
It's simply one of the best books ever
Sitting at #19
On Klecko's all-time best book list

Dear Sjón,
Greetings from St. Paul
I hope you are staying healthy
And content during the pandemic
I am fortunate
I spend six days a week at the bakery
And the rest of my time
Reading and writing
I don't have an MFA, but . . .
I have a desire to continue my struggle
Against ICE and government agencies
That cause suffering
For my Mexican friends
On my project
I have been humbled
By receiving assistance from
George Saunders
Leif Enger
And . . . Jonathan Franzen
Now, I come to you
My final piece of the puzzle

I've read several of your books
BLUE FOX
MOUTH OF THE WHALE
And have CODEX on deck
But MOONSTONE . . . God Damn
It's better than perfect
It's imperfect, raw and unbalanced
Every page I smiled . . .
While cringing with a broken heart
Page One, you threw a brick at us
And never let up
And your closing . . .
Maybe the best close ever

SJÓN—4

I have two questions for you, Sjón
That would help me on my quest . . .

#1—Did you write MOONSTONE
For healing or vindication

#2—What are you reading, writing
During the pandemic

Thanks so much and know . . .
When the world opens up
If you make it to the States
You have a friend in Minnesota

Klecko

SJÓN—5

Dear Klecko,
Thanks for your kind words
About my books
And congratulations on your own book
And the award you won for it
One thing we know here, in Iceland
Good literature can spring from us all
We are all gifted in language at birth
And some of us can't resist
Making that talent work in . . .
Poems, stories and plays

SJÓN—6

Our Nobel Prize winner from 1955
Halldór Laxness, never finished high school
And definitely wasn't worse for it
So, MFAs, and their historical equivalents
Are not what stuff our dreams
Are made of when translated to poetry
I am glad you embraced your talent
And calling to become a poet

As for your questions:
I guess MOONSTONE was partly written
As an accusation directed at a society
That had for too long dictated
Who belongs to its history
And who didn't
It's also a celebration of the queer spirit
And its rebelliousness, its sturdiness
In face of decades, centuries even
Of adversity, and thanks to the LGBTQ+
Community in Iceland
And the rest of the world
For the lesson in human rights
They have given those of us
Born into the privilege
Of not having to fend for
Our right to determine
Who we are

SJÓN—8

During pandemic
I have read less than I imagined I would
Instead I have watched films
I have revisited the classics
At the same time, I have tried to catch up
On what's going on
In contemporary world cinema
I have also been writing for films
And not poetry or prose
Thank you for getting in touch
And the invitation
If I find myself
In your neighbourhood
Good luck with everything
Life, work and play
Warmest regards,
Sjón

DEAR DIARY

Mother, daughter, lean on the counter
KA-CHING . . . cashier rings up
20 dozen donuts, and a cheesecake
I loaded their van
I asked about the donut volume
Mother says . . .
Daughter's getting married tomorrow
Daughter says . . . Who knew
My wedding would be filled
With plague and snow
Both faces were deadpan, until . . .
I announced, a hundred years ago
I got married, and . . .
I don't remember the weather
Or who attended
The only thing I do remember
Is my bride, she was beautiful
Almost as beautiful as today
Mother smiled and said . . . Thanks
Daughter rolled her eyes
But smiled . . . before pulling away
Into an abundance
Of something wetter than snow

BADGER—1

Dear Diary
Shortly after deciding to . . .
Take you into my confidence
It's become obvious
I would write this diary
And name it LINCOLNLAND
Once the vision broke ground
And the ground rules surfaced
I knew how much it would mean
To get feedback about
Robert Bly's poem
"Snowbanks North of the House"
A poem I love
A poem I saw him read
A poem that featured Lincoln
But leaves one wondering, why
I asked my publisher to track down
Thomas R. Smith
Bly's private secretary
3o years running

BADGER—2

Ring–Ring went the phone
Hello, answered Thomas R. Smith
From the comfort of his home
In River Falls, Wisconsin
I asked questions
He returned answers
He asked questions
Because he is gracious
He promised to hook me up
With data, with references
With contact information
Then he suggested
We exchange e-mail addresses
His preferred mode of communication
Since that was that
Wouldn't it just make sense
To send each other a poem

BADGER—3

Dear Diary
Imagine . . .
Sending a poem
To the guy who pored over
Robert Bly's poems for a quarter century
Don't tell anyone
For the first time
In several years
I became indecisive
So I picked up a copy of . . .
HITMAN-BAKER-CASKETMAKER
And rifled through the pages
Eyes closed, squeezed tight
Finger inserted . . .
Landing on . . .
"A Sort of Homecoming"

BADGER—4

The following day
Thomas R. Smith replied
He liked my poem
He liked the tone
It reminded him very much
Of . . .
"Norwegian Wood"
Except, I didn't burn down
The apartment of the girl
I smiled, unaware
Unaware of why I was smiling
I had no idea
What he was talking about
I had no idea
Of his reference point, so . . .
I typed "Norwegian Wood"
Into the Google bar

BADGER—5

Dear Diary
I felt ignorant
I felt stupid
I smiled
"Norwegian Wood" . . .
It's a Beatles song
I smiled
I had written a poem
That linked Thomas R. Smith
To his favorite band

BADGER—6

On the night, of the day
John Lennon . . .
Would have celebrated
His 80th birthday
Thomas R. Smith
Sent me an e-mail
With a poem entitled
"Postwar Sunshine"
A poem that spoke to
England's suffering
Countless catastrophes
But most importantly
Vindication
Vindication in the form
Of the Beatles
Thomas reminded us . . .
Reminded me
Celebration is necessary
Families need to sing louder

BADGER—7

Gosh . . .
I loved "Postwar Sunshine"
It was so well written
I read it out loud
To nobody
In my living room
At least a half-dozen times

BADGER—8

Melville and Tolstoy
Are names to call on
While searching for hope
In the Bardo
But, for those of us
With bones above the ground
How fortunate we are
To be in the now
In the midst of beauty
Let us remember
Bly is best
But Thomas . . . is better
What does it matter
What matters is
They found each other
What matters is
I found Thomas

LEIF ENGER—SEQUEL

Dear Diary . . .
I drove through darkness
Quiet and snow
To reach Park Point
To see Superior
To hear Superior
To see a friend
For a fifth pandemic visit
As the sun came up
I left sourdough loaves as tribute
On boulders of ice
Intersecting the shoreline
One by one
Crows and waves
Pulled bread into the water
I took this as a good sign
Waves roared
The wind picked up
And the temperature began to fall
Just enough to let me know
Today was going to be wonderful

LEIF ENGER—CONCLUSION

Old men never make new friends
But when they do, conversation is great
With lifetimes to discuss
My new friend hit the beach
With an arsenal of kites
So many, I laughed, we laughed
We discussed . . .
Nordic authors
Puppies and publishers
Finally, I confessed, I seldom get envious
But those plot points you told me about
Last time I was here, I want to steal them
Have you considered, you might be Mark Twain
Reincarnated
My new friend mentioned . . .
Today's wind was kind
As we put some kites into the air
Both of us smiled
Realizing, nothing else needed to be discussed

INTERMISSION

LET IT BE—1

1990—
In the middle of August
On the Poet Finley's porch
At a point we considered
If a third Malbec would be opened
"POP" glug-glug-glug was the answer
Street lamps did lamp things
Bugs made bug noises
In the background, the WHITE ALBUM
Provided white noise
A perfect place, a safe space
Safe enough for me to tell the truth
Paul is the Beatles quarterback
His music comes from joy
Lennon, not so much
Finley slid away from the table
Retired without saying goodnight
Leaving me to topple the bottle
While jotting . . .
NOTE TO SELF
Pretty sure my mentor is a Lennon guy

LET IT BE—2

1969—
The Poet Finley lived in Los Angeles
In a commune, in the valley
In and around the Manson Family

The Poet Klecko left Los Angeles
To start a new life
To start elementary school

Early 70's—
The Poet Finley believed
John was the real Beatle
He loved IMAGINE
He loved MIND GAMES
He worked in a newsroom

The Poet Klecko hated the Beatles
It was old people's music
He loved Paul McCartney and Wings
He loved RAM and BAND ON THE RUN
He folded paper airplanes during recess

LET IT BE—3

2015—
The Poet Finley announced
He booked a gig reading poems
In the basement of a bowling alley
In the city of his youth . . .
Cleveland, Ohio
The Poet Finley asked . . .
If I wanted to tag along
Be his opening act
I wouldn't get paid
But he would drive
And he had a case of red in the trunk
In the car, papers crumpled
Stains soaked, music was loud
Halfway between A and B
It occurred to me
And made me curious enough to ask
You only sing along with the Beatles
Why is that . . .
He didn't answer, until he did
They are more than my life's soundtrack
They are my alternate universe
A place where I am allowed to sit in
When Ringo has other engagements

LET IT BE—4

Over the phone
I broke the news to mother
The Poet Finley was dead
There was a pause
I heard her weep
I didn't know how to console her
I improvised . . .
It's good he's gone
He was in pain
Don't cry mother, there was a pause
And another, until she said . . .
I was crying for you
You haven't realized it yet
You're never going to replace him
And a big part of you . . .
Is going to be lonely
Everyday
Until you die

LET IT BE—5

Across St. Paul, I missed him
In my skull, I missed him
But the quiet, that was the worst
For 30 years we spoke
Almost every day, bouncing ideas
Discussing things that gave reason
To think of things to consider
The loss created pain
It might have been better
Had the pain been sharp
Sharp enough to remind me
To look for reason
But everything, or most things
Pain included, became dull
Until, in my skull
It occurred to me
I could rest in Finley's shadow
A feat that required nothing more
Than reading books
About the Beatles

LET IT BE—6

If you discover the Beatles
When you are 57
During a pandemic
The rabbit hole is deep
The free fall confusing
Fall and keep falling
Suspended in air
Impact is eventual . . .
Or is it

LET IT BE—7

I read . . .
Books, books, magazines and books
Coming together, breaking up
Who liked who, who loved who
Who didn't
I read . . .
Books, books, magazines and books
Claims were made
Billy Preston was the 5th
Eric Clapton was the 5th
If it were up to me
I'd choose Billy Preston
For no other reason than
If you're going to be a Beatle
Smiling should be required

LET IT BE—8

I should have known
Why was I surprised
Sir Paul goes bird watching
Between gigs
Thank you, Google
Associated Press too
For providing access
And moments of merit
I should have known
Why wasn't I surprised
When Sir Paul explained
Bird-watching . . .
It's a wonderful way
To chill out

LET IT BE—9

In the rabbit hole
On the internet
I kept reading about the Beatles
I read past the Beatles
Searching out each and every person
Who had a connection
Toward the bottom of the rabbit hole
Twaddle–Jibberish–Clickbait
New York Post, Clickbait
Imagine that
Imagine this, the headline
WIFE OF JOHN LENNON'S KILLER
VISITS HIM FOR SEX AND PIZZA
I didn't want to look
For many reasons
But, I couldn't resist
So . . . I bit

LET IT BE—10

I've been told by my elders
It's sacrilegious to mention the name
Mark David Chapman
I disagree
The world is bigger than the Beatles
Bigger than Lennon
Wasn't it Sherlock Holmes who said . . .
The level of a protagonist
Is often measured by their antagonist
Other than CATCHER IN THE RYE
I didn't know anything about . . .
Mark David Chapman
Least of all . . .
That he had a wife

LET IT BE—11

It's my understanding
It isn't unusual for opportunists
To marry incarcerated killers
Share the spotlight, reap notoriety
Gloria Chapman married . . .
Because she was in love
Every marriage is difficult
Hers was no exception
She remained anchored in Christ
One night, a Monday
While Mark was in New York
She returned home after work
Fixed dinner
Watched "Little House on the Prairie"
The episode where Mary went blind
Midway through, scrawl on the TV announced
John Lennon had been shot
By a Caucasian male
Immediately she assumed it was Mark
Although the moment was dark
Surreal
Gloria Chapman . . .
Remained anchored in Christ

LET IT BE—12

The Bible makes a big deal
Over Moses leading an Exodus
A journey through the desert
A journey of faith
A journey that took 40 years
Although she's too kind to admit it
Moses' jaunt was child's play
Compared to what Gloria endured
While married to a man despised, worldwide
She prayed, never to waiver
While hatred cloaked her family
She prayed, never to buckle
Over 40 years have passed . . .
Over 40 years have passed . . .
A span in which council suggested
Cut the cord, set yourself free
But . . . Gloria clings to MALACHI 2:16
FOR I HATE DIVORCE SAYS THE LORD
With that, she musters hope
Of reunion with her husband
However, until a miracle happens
Gloria Chapman waits alone

LET IT BE—13

For several years I worked with systems
That focused on taking young men
Recently released from incarceration
And placing them in work environments
Where they could thrive
I grew fond of these men
And had a rooting interest
The only difference between them
And me, is they got caught
A circumstance, that manifests
At a higher rate
When you're not white
I grew fond of these men
And made it a point
To single them out on the production floor
Where the crew could witness
Me wrapping my arms around them
Hugging them, and telling them
I love you, we got this, one tribe
They never squirmed
Without exception, they smiled
Before announcing . . .
Old man is crazy as fuck

LET IT BE—14

In my heart, I believe
The result of Chapman's crime
Altered the course of the world
Knocking love off its axis
In my heart, I believe
Mark is repentant
Merits forgiveness
He is partnered with more than Christ
He has Gloria
A woman with character
Noble enough
That if anyone ever writes
A sequel to the Bible
She deserves her own book
Dear Diary . . .
I stand with the Chapmans

LET IT BE—15

Of all the bakers I worked with
Who were formally incarcerated
Very few maintained freedom
Stats on recidivism are mind-blowing
In a nutshell . . .
If you get locked up once
You're going to go back
I thought about it, why . . .
What to do
I wasn't sure, I had an idea
And asked my publisher
To get me an intro
With Gloria Chapman
I wanted to pitch a project

LET IT BE—16

Presto—
My publisher found Gloria
Living in Hawaii
The home base for a prison ministry
Run by Mark and herself
She took the pitch
And asked for my patience
The two prayed over my proposal
Ultimately letting me know
They weren't led in that direction
They thanked me
Said they were sorry to disappoint
But assured me they would be certain
To pray for my endeavors
And my desire to become closer
To Jesus
Gloria said good-bye
But not before
Telling me to read Jeremiah 29:11
Then suggesting
I claim Jeremiah 29:13
For myself

LET IT BE—17

Dear Diary
I have never witnessed America
Having uglier energy
Than during the 2020 Presidential election
The hate
The prejudice
I need to go back to the basics
Start by repenting
God only knows how much
I've contributed to this mess
Return to prayer, Klecko
Pray for family
Pray for America
And don't forget the Chapmans
Put them on top of your prayer list

LET IT BE—18

Dear Diary
I like new books, because they're new
Keeping me up to date, ahead of the pack
I like old books, because they smell old
I like to hold them and wonder who read them
Recently I saw an old book
John Lennon was on the cover
May Pang was on the cover
She was his mistress for 18 months
They loved each other
They saw a UFO, they were happy
I brought the book to the counter
She said, 96 dollars
I recoiled, she smiled, explaining
It's a first edition
It was pulled off the shelves
Yoko took issue
And for reasons I can't explain
I dropped a Benjamin
Eventually understanding . . .
That book was worth every penny

LET IT BE—19

None of my business
None whatsoever
Yet, I made it my own
By surfing Google images
Epicenter of celebrity
Staring at pictures of John
Coupled with Yoko Ono
In tandem with May Pang
Wondering who he loved
Who did John dream about
Didn't matter to me
None of my business
I observed with a neutral heart
Click–Click–Click
Look at that
And that, and that
Oh my

LET IT BE—20

Viewing photographs
It's hard to denote emotion
Posture can be deceiving
Throwing truth off balance
Eyes are the window . . .
To the soul
Look deep and stand reminded
Irrefutable evidence
More often than not
Comes in the form of a glance
Click–Click–Click
Look at that
And that, and that
Dear Diary
I've formed an opinion

LET IT BE—21

Archives, photographs
Do your own research
I did mine, now I know
Yoko seldom looks at John
Passion never surfaces
But, maybe on a good day
Mutual gain is collected
If a tacit agreement
Stays in place
May Pang looks at him, in him
She swoons
Practically melting, floating
I'm not sure John understood
Every time May Pang looked his way
He had never been more visible

LET IT BE—22

I read a book, I read a blog
Indicating during his final years
John replaced music with bread baking
His guitar served no purpose
He hung it on the wall
The only thing that got him off
Flour, water, salt and yeast
Flour, water, salt and yeast
It's been reported
John Lennon said . . .
Making good bread
Is something even a Beatle
Can be proud of

LET IT BE—23

I wanted to hear more
About Lennon the baker
I asked my publisher
To get me an introduction with May Pang
Presto . . .
Between what would have been
John's 80th birthday
And May's 70th birthday
A flurry of e-mails was exchanged

LET IT BE—24

It started in typical fashion
Chit Chat—Small Talk
We shared Los Angeles
Both of us had lived there
Chit Chat—Chit Chat
May's first car . . .
A 1968 rust-colored Plymouth Barracuda
My first car . . .
A 69 gold Barracuda
Chit Chat—Small Talk
We each had a son
Living in the same Midwestern city
Conversation was relaxed
Curiosity appropriate
So, I asked, about John
About his baking
About the UFO
They saw outside their penthouse
Crickets . . .
Chit Chat—What's That
Small Talk—Small Talk
And nothing beyond

LET IT BE—25

For the fifth consecutive Sunday
My mother the Mystic . . .
Called and asked what I was doing
I explained
I work every Sunday mother
She explained
Old people don't use calendars
Days are the same
I told her I had to go
She told me about her cats
I told her I had to go
She complained about the Russians next door
I insisted I had to go
I had to load the oven
She told me she discovered a secret pond
Containing swans, swans are beautiful
Had I ever seen a swan, if not, I should
Because they are delightful
Then she paused and asked . . .
What's new with you

LET IT BE—26

I told her about May Pang
About our conversations
How she seemed to enjoy
Talking about bakeries
Talking about baguettes
As long as the topic was food
Chit Chat
But when I brought up John
Not a word . . .
Mother interrupted
As our family is apt to do
Reminding me . . . Sometimes memories have teeth
  that bite
After work, I sent May Pang an e-mail
Apologizing for my poor form
And announced I was withdrawing
My questions about John
Almost immediately she replied . . .
Talk to you soon

LET IT BE—27

Amidst a winter night's dream
Cold, cold without snow
Under an exhausted sky
Stars blinked dull
I stood alone
Or so I thought
On a rooftop
In London town
The band was gone
Their gear remained
I picked up Paul's base
Held it, not knowing what to do
I don't play bass, and am unfamiliar
With the language of music
But I know what a piano sounds like
Behind me, someone was plunking keys
I turned, I saw, I smiled
A silhouette
Bent over, lurching forward
Making music
It was Lincoln

LET IT BE—28

His face had a blue hue
Not eerie, but unnerving
I considered factors
Moonlight above
Streetlights below
Truthfully, it didn't matter
He played the piano
Nimble flourishes
Impressive dexterity
All this from . . .
A guy with sodbuster hands
Flourishes segued to scales
Scales turned into song
It was cold
Lincoln rocked slow
Bobbing, up and down
Until he stopped
Acknowledged me with a glance
Then he began to frown
Before playing a melancholy version of
LET IT BE

As Lincoln played . . .
His hands trembled, eyes hollowed
At first, I couldn't discern
The source of his pain
During the chorus, he changed the lyric to . . .
"THERE WON'T BE AN ANSWER
LET IT BE"
When the song was over
He remained silent, looking at me
Looking puzzled
The reaction caught me off guard
I was ill prepared and responded
By shrugging, and asking . . .
What?
Lincoln looked thoughtful
While carefully selecting a response
He said . . .
Everyone else has moved on
The Beatles, the bakers, me too
I think it would be a good idea
If you did the same

LET IT BE—30

The shame was more than I could handle
I had overstayed my welcome
Lincoln sat motionless, staring
I didn't know how to exit
I froze, I wasn't certain
What decorum was appropriate
I didn't know how to exit
Do I wave
Do I get to say good-bye
Fearful of making matters worse
I said nothing and walked away
As I approached the fire escape
Lincoln called my name
I turned, he grinned
But . . .
Just as he was about to speak
I woke up

LET IT BE—31

In bed, numb
I didn't stir
In bed, numb
The dream remained foggy
I was tempted
To reach for a notebook and pen
I didn't stir
Instead, I did my best
To reel the dream in
Was there a message
A point
I didn't stir
But, I did smile
Realizing . . .
It was time
To stop chasing ghosts
Instead
I would get by
With a little help
From my friends

BOOK CLUB QUESTIONS

1. During the pandemic, Klecko dared to reach out to heroes that had impact on his life. Which of your heroes would you contact if you had the courage of Klecko?

2. This entire book is a quest based on a dream. How have you paid attention to your own dreams?

3. Klecko saw the ghost of Abraham Lincoln in Clermont, Iowa. Have you ever seen a ghost? Does the thought of seeing a ghost comfort you or frighten you?

4. In addition to all of the celebrity cameos in LINCOLNLAND, Klecko writes about his encounters with a variety of birds. Can you name all of the birds featured in this book?

5. Reflecting on all of the stories in this book, which one surprised you the most? Which one moved you the most? And which one made you smile?

6. Have you ever kept a diary? What types of memories did you record there?

7. Based on everything you read in LINCOLNLAND, what is one word you would use to describe Klecko? Why?

8. John or Paul?

Hey, it's me Klecko . . .
I kinda thought this book was over
But while you guys were reading
Book club questions
It occurred to me I have put together
A wonderful diary of short stories
Wonderful is good, but it isn't perfect
Then it occurred to me it would be perfect
If I could get my friend Thomas R. Smith
To present his poem
"Postwar Sunshine"
If you will indulge me
For a brief moment
I'm going to call Thomas
And see if he will favor us
By closing out this book
Gosh . . . I hope he says yes
Hold on . . .

TICK–TOCK
TICK–TOCK
RING–RING
BLAH-BLAH-BLAH
BLAH-BLAH-BLAH
BLAH
REALLY, YES
EXCELLENT
YES
THANK YOU, THOMAS
SO MUCH

OK, friends
Thomas is in
He's going to drive this book home
The very moment
You turn the page

POSTWAR SUNSHINE

"Liverpool, that great matrix of Anglo-Celtic alchemy."
—*Mark Lewisohn*

Imagine your grandparents carrying across
the Irish Sea the deprivations of famine,
behind that the cruelties of Cromwell.
Imagine your parents' hand-to-mouth scuffle
in that port city, serving the commodious
god of the Merseyside docks and warehouses,
the merciless gospel of capital.
Then imagine the war finding you, again,
this time Hitler pounding that hub of trade
and commerce, killing thousands from the air,
the living forced underground, masking their light.
Imagine afterward a habitual fear of the sky,
of raising too high a profile to the predators.
Imagine growing into one's body
in a womb that has taken in that trouble.
Imagine your playground the rubbled buildings,
childhood games in the unreconstructed "bommies,"
later the Teds like unexorcised revenants
on the mean streets of Speke, the Dingle.
Yet good things still happen after a war—
against the past, against the odds. Gray skies
must break, sun suggest again the contour
of what was lost, what is worth recovering.
Celebration not only possible again but
necessary, families sing the louder,
each member stepping up to take their turn.

While the parents juggle extra jobs to feed
their children, there are those children fed
on music, implausibly raising the spare
quid for a plywood guitar, the second-
hand drumset, bussing across town to learn
a new chord, rummaging the record shops
for the outrageous new rock and roll import.
Go back and listen to them again—the boy
who lost his mother to cancer, the boy
who lost his mother to the ordinary violence
of the combustion engine—and you may
hear in their voices, in the furious joy
of their playing in defiance of all this
their desperation and style, how they rose
each of them from some gritty seed-bed
on stalks tough and resilient enough to become
the unlikely sunflowers we know them as,
each sadness-tempered, who with the alchemy
of song transformed the gray dross of the given—
mundane Strawberry Field and Penny Lane—
into a gift for the world, that the sun may
resume its indiscriminate work of healing
the brokenness historical trauma inflicts on us,
which we then inflict upon our children.

NOTE: Although my reading of numerous books about the Beatles over decades, not to mention even longer immersion in the Beatles' music itself, underlies and informs "Postwar Sunshine," I'd be remiss not to mention a chief source for the Liverpool background of my poem, Mark Lewisohn's *Tune In*, the first volume of his mammoth definitive "biography" of the group, *The Beatles: All These Years*. Liverpool's "Anglo-Celtic alchemy" really is the matrix of the Beatles' deep and enduring appeal to audiences across almost any kind of divide we can imagine, and Mr. Lewisohn's detailed prose brings that matrix sensorily alive for his readers.

I'm indebted to him for supplying specific textures of postwar Liverpool that save my poem from being a paean of more general, if heart-felt praise.

—Thomas R. Smith

Klecko

Winner of a 2020 Midwest Book Award, Klecko is a Master Bread Baker. He's spent close to four decades designing product lines across the Twin Cities. Currently he and the Russian Supermodel live in a mansion catty-corner from the home where F. Scott Fitzgerald wrote his first novel. He enjoys Nordic authors, Rolling Stones albums and Dora Maar paintings.

To see photos from the LINCOLNLAND Virtual Diary, visit the LINCOLNLAND page on Facebook.

A Note on the Type

The text of this book was set in Didot,
a revival of the typefaces of the Parisian
type-founder Firmin Didot (1764–1836).